TREES

A PHOTOGRAPHIC GUIDE
TO NATIVE NORTH AMERICAN TREES

TREES

A PHOTOGRAPHIC GUIDE
TO NATIVE NORTH AMERICAN TREES

GRACE MOORE

© 2022 Moseley Road Inc.
www.moseleyroad.com

President: Sean Moore
Production Director: Adam Moore

Managing Editor: Jill Hamilton
Design and Picture Research: Tina Vaughan

ISBN: 9781626692183

Printed and bound in China

10 9 8 7 6 5 4 3

CONTENTS

CONTENTS

INTRODUCTION

Trees are a source of unlimited inspiration and fascination, whether they grace city streets and urban parks or are encountered in the country, on hikes, or long-distance expeditions into the wilderness. A firm count of 58,497 species of trees worldwide was determined by the UK-based Botanical Gardens Conservation International in 2021. Of these, 841 species are native to the U.S., and 125 species are profiled in detail in this book. The profiles show the whole tree in its environment and describe some of the many ways in which trees can be differentiated: overall shape and growth pattern; size; bark; leaves, flowers, and fruit; habitat and distribution. Trees as we think of them consist of roots, trunk, branches, and, depending on the season and type of tree, leaves, flowers, and fruits of various shapes, sizes, and colors.

Despite the many visual characters that can be used to help identify trees and distinguish one species from another, they are classified as either softwoods or hardwoods according a microscopic characteristic: the seed coating or lack thereof. A tree is a softwood if the seed shell has no coating, such as the seeds in a pine cone, but is a hardwood if it does have a coating, which may be in the form of a fruit or a shell, or even just a winged samara. The botanical names for these two groups are gymnosperm, meaning "naked seed," and angiosperm, for "vessel seed."

Although there are exceptions in both groups, softwoods—gymnosperms—are generally evergreen while hardwoods—angiosperms—are deciduous.

Softwoods are also known as conifers for the cone receptacle that holds and protects the naked seeds on leaflike structures called bracts until they are shed is termed a cone. Only yellow pines produce the "typical" pine cone—but all other forms produced by conifers are cones but in less recognizable forms.

The softwoods in North America are classified into three families: the Pinaceae, or pine family, the Cupressaceae, the cypresses, as well as the trees in the subgroup Taxodiaceae such as the Coast redwood; and the Taxaceae, with just one species in North America, the American yew. The Pinaceae family, in turn, is subdivided into 11 genera, four of which occur in North America: *Pinus*, *Abies*, *Picea*, and *Larix*. The genus *Pinus* has 115 species worldwide, 49 of which are native to North America. The *Abies* (firs) have 49 species worldwide with 9 native to North America; *Picea* (spruces) have 35 worldwide and seven in North America; and *Larix* (larches), which is the only deciduous conifer, has ten species worldwide, of which two are found in North America. All have needles althouth they are attached differently to the branch, but only

Pinus bears the traditional cone, angled down. The *Abies* are recognized by their large cones, growing upward, that disintegrate as they mature and the seeds are released, while *Picea* cones are generally smooth and angled downward.

The Cupressaceae family, or cypresses, although smaller in number than the Pinaceae, has a wider distribution: roughly 140 species, in 30 genera, are found throughout the Northern and Southern Hemispheres, from arctic Norway to southern Chile, and in China it reaches the highest altitude—17,060 feet (5,200 m)—of any woody plant. The four Cupressaceae genera native to North America are *Chaemacyparis* (false cypresses), *Juniperus* (junipers), *Thuja* (whitecedar and redcedar), and *Sequoia* (redwood). Only the *Sequoia* has needle-shaped foliage; the others have compressed, scalelike leaves. Their cones are all different, from the globose form produced by *Chaemacyparis*, to the berries of *Juniperus*, the upright woody version of *Thuja*, and the globose collection of tiny winged seeds of *Sequoia*, so diminutive compared to the giant redwood that produces them.

All hardwoods are characterized by flat, veined leaves, most of which change color before falling, generally in the autumn, unlike the evergreen, needle-shaped foliage of most softwoods. The diversity of hardwoods is far greater than that of softwoods because of the variation in reproductive strategies that is facilated by protection of the seed by a specialized fruit. Depending on the nature of the fruit, hardwood—angiosperm—seed may be dispersed by wind or water, or digested and excreted by animals that feed on the fruit. The seed coatings of hardwoods include winged samaras, which are barely more than the seeds themselves; acorns; fruiting catkins; pods; nuts; berries; and drupes.

Of 132 species of maples (the genus *Acer* in the family Sapindaceae), most have palmate leaves, Maple fruits, called samaras, carry pairs of seeds encased in papery wings, which are dispersed by the wind. Most maples have both male and female flowers on the same tree (monoecious) and are therefore self-fertilizing, although some are on separate trees (diecious). The 150 species in the birch family are easily recognized by their simple, pinnate leaves, most of which are either

toothed or serrated. Male and female flowers are borne in separate catkins but on the same tree, so all birch trees are monoecious and can self-fertilize. The oak genus (*Quercus*), in the family Fagaceae, has some 500 species that are primarily native to the Northern Hemisphere, classified as either red or white oaks depending on physical characteristics of their acorns.

Hardwoods such as the legumes are recognized by compound pinnate leaves and seeds that are encased in a fleshy pod; the seeds are disseminated by livestock grazing on the pods. The fruits of some hardwoods, such as the sweetgum and the sycamore family, are formed from tightly packed individual seed packets, which disintegrate when the fruit matures in the fall; both of these groups are easily recognizable because of their distinctive, lobed leaves.

The *magnolia*s, in the *Magnolia* genus of the family Magnoliaceae, number about 210 species distributed worldwide. It is an ancient genus that, based on its flower structure, is believed to have evolved to be pollinated by beetles rather than by bees. The fruit, which resembles a pine cone, conceals black seeds that are encased in a fleshy aril that looks like a red or orange berry.

SOFTWOOD TREES

PINACEAE

The pine family is the largest family of softwoods, with more than 200 species distributed over most of the Northern Hemisphere. Nearly all are tall trees with a conical to pyramidal form and needlelike leaves.

The egg-shaped seed cones produced by the yellow pines of the genus *Pinus* are the type recognized as a traditional pine cone but there is a lot of variety in shape, color, and growth form both within and between species.

ABIES (FIR)

FORM Firs are conical or pyramidal in shape, most with straight trunks, and some attaining heights of 200 feet or more. Close up, the short needles can be seen, each one fastened individually to the twig.

REPRODUCTION The female cones grow upward, looking like large cylindrical candles in the top few feet of the tree. The winged seeds are released when the cones disintegrate at maturity.

PICEA (SPRUCE)

FORM Spruces have a crown that is conical in younger trees, becoming more cylindrical as they age, with whorled branches. The needles are four-sided and individually attached to the branches by peglike structures.

REPRODUCTION The cones are erect, similar to those of the firs, but when they are pollinated they become pendulous (hang downward). The pollen grains that are released are double-winged.

LARIX (LARCH)

PINUS (PINE)

FORM Larches are generally tall, slendar trees, narrowly conic at the crown, with the top branches upswept but the side branches drooping. The slender needle-like leaves turn yellow in the fall before they are shed.

REPRODUCTION Each cone has 40–80 seed scales, and when the cones open on maturity, a seed is released from each of the scales. Leaves are fastened in groups of ten or more in fascicles.

FORM All pine trees produce one or more tight rings of branches every year; over time, lower whorls drop off. The bark shows sticky secretions because pines respond to injury by secreting a resin.

REPRODUCTION The cones show wide variation in both size and shape. Some release their seeds at maturation while others are serotinous: the resin protecting the cone must be melted before it can open.

Average height: 80–110 ft (24–33.5 m)
Average trunk diameter: 2–4 ft
(61–122 cm)
Lifespan: 80–115 years

PACIFIC SILVER FIR
Abies amabilis

Abies amabilis, also known as the Pacific silver fir, white fir, red fir, lovely fir, Amabilis fir, Cascades fir, or silver fir, is a high-elevation evergreen native to the Pacific Northwest. It is one of four true fir species found in the region. This large tree grows straight with a spirelike crown that becomes flat topped with age. The tree's wood is soft and is used as a source of pulp for making paper. Silver firs are sometimes planted as ornamental trees in large parks, although their need for cool, humid summers limits the areas where they will thrive.

INTERESTING FACTS

• The wood is soft and is often used for paper making, packing crates, and other cheap construction work.

• Native people used the boughs for bedding or floor coverings, chewed the pitch as gum, and used the soft, brittle wood as firewood.

• The epithet *amabilis* means "lovely."

Bark: On young trees, the bark is silvery-gray, thin, and mostly smooth with resin blisters. As the tree ages, the bark will darken and break into scales, distinguishing it from the furrowed bark on other firs.

HABITAT AND DISTRIBUTION

Foliage: The needles on a Pacific silver fir are dark matte green on top with white lines underneath. They grow forward and upward from the branch and range from 1–2 in (2.5–5 cm) long and 2 mm wide.

Habitat
The pacific silver fir grows at mid to higher elevations in temperate rain forests with relatively high precipitation. It is shade-tolerant, sensitive to drought, and requires cool, humid summers. It often grows in pure stands of trees and sometimes alongside subalpine fir and mountain hemlock.

Cones: The cones sit upright on the branch and change color from green to purple upon maturity. They range in length from 3.5–7 in (9–18 cm). Like other firs, cones fall apart upon maturity—about 6 months after pollination.

Distribution
As the name suggests, this tree is native to the Pacific Northwest, specifically in the Pacific Coast Ranges and the Cascade Range from the southeast of Alaska, through western British Columbia, Washington, and Oregon, to the northwest of California.

Avg height: 46–66 ft (14–20 m)
Avg trunk diameter: 12–18 in (30–45 cm)
Lifespan: 150–200 years

Bark: Bark is gray, thin, smooth, and covered with many resin blisters that tend to spray when ruptured. As the tree ages, the bark will break into rough, irregular brownish scales.

Foliage: The flat needles are about 0.6–1.2 in (1.5–3 cm) long, growing spirally along the shoot. The top of the needle is a shiny dark green while the underside is pale with a few white lines. Needles are shorter and thicker the higher up they are on the tree.

Cones: The seed cones are 1.5–3 inches (3.8–7.6 cm) long, and stand erect on branches. They are dark purple in color, but ripen to brown, and disintegrate to release the winged seeds in September.

BALSAM FIR
Abies balsamea

Abies balsamea, commonly called the balsam fir, balm of Gilead, northern balsam, silver pine, or blister fir, is a medium-sized North American evergreen. Its symmetrical, spirelike crown, dark green color, and aromatic foliage have made it a popular Christmas tree for hundreds of years. This plant has been widely used medicinally by various Native Americans for hundreds of years, treating a variety of ailments including heart disease, colds, kidney pains, sore throat, rheumatic joints, headache, coughs, boils, bruises, sprains, and colic.

INTERESTING FACTS

• The resin from this tree has been historically used as a glue for glasses, as an optical instrument component, and to mount thin specimens under microscopes.

• The balsam fir is extremely cold-hardy, being known to survive temperatures as low as -49°F (-45 °C).

• Chemicals in the needles mimic a growth hormone that interferes with normal insect metamorphosis, giving it a unique defense against insect feeders.

HABITAT AND DISTRIBUTION

Habitat
Balsam firs tend to grow in cool climates and prefer consistent moisture at their roots. They typically grow in swamps, flats, and hardwood sloping forests and mountain tops. In swamp and mountain top habitats, balsam firs tend to grow densely and slowly, while flats and hardwood slope habitats lead to fast, tall, and large growth.

Distribution
The balsam fir is widely distributed in northeastern North America. In Canada, the tree's range extends from Newfoundland and Labrador west through the more northerly portions of Quebec and Ontario. In the United States, it can be found from Minnesota east to Maine, and south in the Appalachian mountains to West Virginia.

WHITE FIR

Abies concolor

Avg height: 80–195 ft (25–60 m)
Avg trunk diameter: 40–80 in (101–203 cm)
Lifespan: 300–400 years

Abies concolor, also called the white fir or concolor fir, is a shade-tolerant conifer native to the mountains of western North America. It is a hardy tree that tolerates a wide range of conditions including drought, heat, and cold temperatures, being particularly well adapted for germination and survival in deep snow. The wood of the white fir is considered one of the most important commercial softwoods in the lumber industry due to its light weight, resistance to split, and ability to hold nails. It is also popularly used as a Christmas decoration due to its excellent needle retention and abundance.

Bark: Young white fir bark is similar to the bark of the Balsam fir in that it is smooth, gray, and covered with resin-filled blisters. On mature trees, it becomes very thick—4–7 in (10–18 cm)—and deeply furrowed into hard wide ridges and plates.

Needles: The flat, bluish-green needles are 1–2.4 in (2.5–6 cm) long and feature two pale blue-white bands on the underside. They are slightly notched to bluntly pointed at the tip. Leaves grow spirally on the shoot, with each leaf variably twisted at the base so they all lie in either two flat ranks on either side of the shoot.

Cones: Cones are 3–5 in (8–12 cm) long and are found on the upper part of the tree. They are green or purple in color, ripening to a pale brown. Each features 100–150 scales, on a short scale bract. Like most firs, the winged seeds are released at maturity—about 6 months after pollination.

INTERESTING FACTS

• The white fir has one of the largest ranges of any of the commercial western firs.

• White fir Christmas trees require 6 to 9 years to produce a 6 ft (1.8 m) tree.

• Initial growth rate is usually very slow up to about 30 years, then growth accelerates markedly.

HABITAT AND DISTRIBUTION

Habitat
The white fir grows in moderately humid climates with long winters. It thrives in areas with ample moisture, preferring areas where precipitation is 36–75 in (91–190 cm) annually, although it has been known to survive in drier habitats as well.

Distribution
White fir can be found in the mountains of western North America from the southern Cascades of Oregon, throughout California, and into the Sierra de San Pedro Mártir; east in southern Idaho to Wyoming; and south throughout the Rocky Mountains in Utah and Colorado, and into the mountain ranges of southern Arizona, New Mexico, and northern Mexico.

Avg height: 30–50 ft (10–15 m)
Avg trunk diameter: 16–20 in (40–50 cm)
Lifespan: 100–150 years

Bark: The bark of the Fraser fir is thin, smooth, and grayish-brown. Like other firs, it contains numerous resinous blisters on juvenile trees, which become fissured and scaly in maturity.

Foliage: The bluish-green needles are 0.4–0.9 in (1–2.3 cm) long, are rounded or slightly notched at the tip, and feature two silvery-white stripes on their underside. They are arranged spirally on the twigs but twisted at their bases to form two rows on each twig.

Cones: The cones of the Fraser fir grow to be 1.5–2.75 in (3.5–7 cm) long. They start out dark purple, turning pale brown at maturity, and feature long reflexed green, yellow, or pale purple bract scales. Cones disintegrate when mature to release the seeds.

FRASER FIR
Abies fraseri

Abies fraseri, commonly called the Fraser fir (sometimes misspelled "Frasier," "Frazer," or "Frazier"), is a species of fir native to the Appalachian Mountains of the Southeastern United States. It is named after Scottish botanist Jon Fraser (1750-1811), a collector of North American plants who first introduced it to European cultivation. The crown is conical, with straight branches that are either horizontal or angled slightly upward from the trunk. Young trees are very dense and tend to open up with maturity. The strong fragrance of the Fraser fir has been said to resemble turpentine. It is not an important source of timber, but its shape, color, natural density, and ability to retain needles make it another popular Christmas tree choice.

INTERESTING FACTS

• In the past, the Fraser fir was sometimes called the "she-balsam" because resin could be "milked" from its bark blisters, as opposed to the "he balsam" (red spruce), which could not be milked.

• Fraser fir is monoecious, meaning that both male and female cones occur on the same tree.

• Fraser fir has been used more times as the White House Christmas tree than any other tree.

HABITAT AND DISTRIBUTION

Habitat
These trees occur at high elevation, from 3,900–6,684 ft (1,200–2,037 m), and live in acidic moist but well-drained sandy loam. The climate is cool and moist, with short, cool summers and cold winters with heavy snowfall. It usually grows in mixed stands alongside red spruce (*Picea rubens*).

Distribution
The Fraser fir is under threat from climate change and is considered an endangered species. Its relatively small range is restricted to the southeastern Appalachian Mountains in southwestern Virginia, western North Carolina, and eastern Tennessee.

Avg height: 130–230 ft (40–70 m)
Avg trunk diameter: 62–78 in
(155–198 cm)
Lifespan: 250–300 years

Bark: On younger trees, the bark is grayish-green, thin and smooth, and covered with resin-blisters. The bark thickens as it matures, becoming grayish brown and patchy with flattened, ridged wrinkles. The inner bark is purple-red.

Cones: The bluish-red or purple cones are 2–4 in (5–10 cm) long and grow upright in the tops of trees. They become purplish-green to green at maturity. Like most other firs, the winged seeds are released at maturity—about 6 months after pollination.

Foliage: The glossy dark yellow-green needles are 1–2 in (2.5–5 cm) long, and are slightly notched at the tip. The two stomata stripes on the underside are green-white. Like other firs, they are arranged spirally on the twigs but twisted at their bases to form two rows on each twig.

GRAND FIR
Abies grandis

Abies grandis, otherwise known as the grand fir, giant fir, lowland white fir, great silver fir, western white fir, Vancouver fir, or Oregon fir, is a large evergreen and one of the tallest species of fir. It is native to the Pacific Northwest and northern California of North America. When young, the grand fir grows in a near-perfect conical Christmas tree shape with branches that spread and droop. The crown becomes round-topped or scraggly with age. The lumber is lightweight and not very strong but is often used as flooring due to its resistance to splitting and splintering. It is more often used as pulp in paper-making.

INTERESTING FACTS

• The bark has medicinal properties and was used by some Indigenous peoples of the Plateau for treating colds and fever. The Okanagan-Colville tribe used it to treat general feelings of weakness.

• The grand fir is thought to be the tallest *Abies* species in the world.

• The grand fir will often hybridize with the white fir (*Abies concolor*), which it commonly grows alongside in the wild.

HABITAT AND DISTRIBUTION

Habitat
The grand fir is shade tolerant, though it grows more quickly when growing in the open. It grows from moist river valleys to dry rain-shadow forests. It does best in areas where summers are mild and winters are cool and wet.

Distribution
The Grand fir has a split distribution. It grows along the Pacific Coast from southern British Columbia, throughout most of western Washington and Oregon, south to the coastline in northern California. It can also be found in the Rocky Mountains of northern Idaho and western Montana.

CALIFORNIA RED FIR
Abies magnifica

Abies magnifica, also called California red fir, red fir, or silvertip fir, is a western North American fir, native to the mountains of southwest Oregon and California. They tend to be symmetrical in shape, with strong but short branches that spread from the trunk in rings and have a narrow crown. The California red fir gets its name from the reddish-brown color of the bark on mature trees. As lumber, it is commonly grouped together with other species of fir and hemlock and sold under the more generic label "hem-fir," and is used for general structural purposes.

Avg height: 130–200 ft (40–60 m)
Avg trunk diameter: 78–102 in (198–259 cm)
Lifespan: 250–400 years

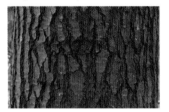

Bark: The bark of young trees is thin, smooth, gray, and covered with resin blisters. As the tree matures, it becomes thick and deeply furrowed in narrow ridges, turning reddish-brown in color.

Foliage: The needles are 0.8–1.4 in (2–3.5 cm) long, glaucous blue-green on top with strong white bands at the bottom and an acute tip. They are arranged spirally on the shoot, but twisted slightly to be upcurved above the shoot.

Cones: The cones grow upright on the upper branches and range from 4–9 in (10–23 cm) long. They are typically yellow-green when young, ripening brown and disintegrating to release the winged seeds in the fall.

INTERESTING FACTS

• Early California mountaineers prepared their beds by cutting and overlapping rows of the plush, fragrant boughs.

• The trunk of the California red fir tends to be brittle and is prone to windfall.

• A dwarf version of this fir, colloquially called "Nana," is much sought after as a Christmas tree.

HABITAT AND DISTRIBUTION

Habitat
It is a high elevation tree, preferring the frigid soils of the higher mountains between 4,600–8,900 ft (1,400–2,700 m). It prefers well-drained, acidic, moist soil and typically thrives in areas with deep snowpacks in the winter, with annual precipitation ranging from 40–50 in (100–127 cm) per year.

Distribution
California red fir occurs in the Sierra Nevada from Kern County, California, north to the southern Cascade Range of Oregon and in the Coast Ranges from Lake County, California, north to the Klamath Ranges. It can also be found in extreme western Nevada. than on the coastal side.

Avg height: 130–230 ft (40–70 m)
Avg trunk diameter: 45–60 in (114–152 cm)
Lifespan: 350–400 years

Bark: The bark on young noble firs is smooth and gray with resin blisters. As the tree matures, it becomes thick and deeply furrowed in narrow ridges, turning reddish-brown in color.

Foliage: The needles are blue-green in color with whitish stomatal lines on both upper and lower surfaces. They are 1–1.4 in (2.5–3.5 cm) long, spreading in rows, and rounded or slightly notched at the tip. Needles are flat on lower branches but conspicuously 4-sided on mid and upper branches.

Cones: Cones are 5.5–9.8 in (14–25 cm) long, green when young, and purple-brown when ripe. Bracts are prominent, long, pointed (although shorter than on *Abies magnifica*), and reflexed so as to hide scales. Cones disintegrate to release the winged seeds in the fall.

NOBLE FIR
Abies procera

Abies procera, known as the noble fir or sometimes red fir, is a western North American fir native to the Pacific Northwest. It is very closely related to the California red fir (*Abies magnifica*) and can be distinguished from this counterpart by the presence of a groove along the midrib on the upper side of the needles. Similar to the California red fir, it is a symmetrically pyramidal to narrow tree with blue-green needles. It grows at high altitudes, typically occurring at 980–4,920 ft (300–5,000 m). Its wood is used for general structural purposes and paper manufacture. It is also used as a Christmas tree.

INTERESTING FACTS

• Noble fir can establish quickly and is often used for reforestation of high-elevation stock in British Columbia.

• This tree roots deeply, making it resistant to wind damage.

• Its wood is the strongest of the true firs. It is a specialty wood used for ladder rails and airplane construction because of its high strength to weight ratio.

HABITAT AND DISTRIBUTION

Habitat
Noble fir grows in young, mixed stands alongside the Pacific silver fir, Douglas fir, and sometimes the western hemlock and mountain hemlock. They occur in a maritime climate with cool summers and mild, wet winters, and require cool, moist, well-drained soil.

Distribution
Noble fir grows at elevations above 2,000 feet in the Coast Range and the Cascades. Although they don't usually grow in pure stands, large numbers can be found on Saddle Mountain near Seaside, and at the top of Larch Mountain and Nesmith Point in the Columbia Gorge.

FIR CONES AND NEEDLES

The true firs—some 50 species of conifers in the genus *Abies* of the pine family—are found in montane and boreal habitats across the Northern Hemisphere. They can be distinguished from other conifers by their distinctive leaves and upward-growing cones. Each flat, needle-shaped leaf is attached individually to the branch and many are arranged spirally. Unlike most other pines, the large female cones grow up from the branch rather than down, and then disintegrate after they are fertilized, releasing the winged seeds. They change in color, green when immature but deep purple or brown when mature, and can be distinguished by size, color, and whether the bracts are long and extend outside the cone, or are hidden inside the cone. All firs bear both male and female flowers but, because the female flowers are far above the male, at the top of the trees where the cones later develop, they are usually fertilized by pollen from another tree.

The Douglas-Fir is not a true fir, being in the genus *Pseudotsuga.* However, its needles resemble those of the firs but completely encircle the twigs,

Pacific Silver Fir *Abies amabilis*
Needles: 0.75 in (2 cm), mostly two-ranked, notched at tip, flattened, dark green, arranged spirally, each leaf twisted at base so none lie below the twig . Cones: 4 in (10 cm), broad, dark purple, scale bracts short and hidden in closed cone,

Balsam Fir *Abies balsamea*
Needles: flattened at tip; 1 in (2.5 cm), blunt, dark-green above; arranged spirally but bases twisted so they seem to be in two horizontal rows on either side of the twig. Cones: to 3 in (7.5 cm), grayish-purple or purplish-green, ripening to brown.

Grand Fir *Abies grandis*
Needles: 2-ranked; 1.25 in (3.2 cm), notched at tip, arranged spirally, twisted at the the base so they lie in two flat ranks on either side of the shoot. Cones: 2.5 in (6.4 cm), green, purple, or blue-gray; bracts short and hidden in cone.

California Red Fir *Abies magnifica*
Needles: 1 in (2.5 cm), arranged spirally, twisted slightly s-shaped so they look upcurved along shoot; flattened, pointed tip. Cones: 7 in (18 cm), purple to greenish-brown; bracts hidden in cone..

White Fir *Abies concolor*
Needles: relatively long, 2 in (5 cm), curved, glaucous gray-green above and below, each twisted at base so none lie below the twig, two stomata bands on underside of leaf sparse, rounded tip. Cones: 4 in (10 cm), olive-green or purple.

Fraser Fir *Abies fraseri*
Needles: arranged spirally, twisted at base to form two rows on each twig; rounded or notched at tip, glaucous-green above. Cones: 2 in (5 cm), dark purple, turn pale brown with green, yellow, or pale purple bracts.

Noble Fir *Abies procera*
Needles: 0.75 in (2 cm), arranged spirally, twisted slightly so they look upcurved along shoot. Cones: 5 in (12.7 cm), purple scales of cone almost totally hidden by yellow-green bract scales.

Douglas-Fir *Pseudotsuga menziesii*
Needles: totally encircle the twigs, Cones: the female cones hang down, and do not disintegrate after the seeds are released. The large bract above each scale has been compared to the back half of a mouse, with tail and back legs.

DOUGLAS-FIR
Pseudotsuga menziesii

Average height: 70–330 ft (for Coastal variety)
Avg trunk diameter: 4.9–6.6 ft (1.5–2 m)
Lifespan, Coastal variety: 500 years, max. up to 1,300 years
Lifespan, Rocky Mountain variety: max. 400 years

Bark: The bark on young trees is thin, smooth, gray, with resin blisters. mature trees have very thick, corky bark with distinctive, deep vertical fissures.

Plentiful cones: The Douglas fir cones are nearly always intact and plentiful both on and under the tree.

Food source: The Douglas squirrel harvests and hoards great quantities of Douglas-fir cones, and also consumes mature pollen cones, the inner bark, terminal shoots, and developing young needles. Douglas-fir seeds are an extremely important food source for small mammals such as moles, shrews, and chipmunks, which consume an estimated 65% of each annual seed crop.

The Douglas-fir (*Pseudotsuga menziesii*) is an evergreen conifer in the pine family, *Pinaceae,* that is native to western North America. The common name is misleading because it is not a true fir, that is, not a member of the genus *Abies*. It is also known as Douglas spruce, Oregon pine, and Columbian pine. There are three varieties: Coast Douglas-fir (*P. menziesii var. menziesii*), Rocky Mountain Douglas-fir (*P. menziesii var. glauca*) with a more inland range, and Mexican Douglas-fir (*P. menziesii var. lindleyana*), sometimes considered a separate species. The common name honors David Douglas, a Scottish botanist and collector who first reported the extraordinary nature and potential of the species. Douglas-firs vary hugely in height; the coastal variety lives far longer than the inland, and attains far greater size.

INTERESTING FACTS

• The Douglas-fir is not a true fir (*Abies*), spruce (*Picea*), or pine (*Pinus*). It is also not a hemlock; the genus name *Pseudotsuga* means "false hemlock."

• The genome of Douglas-fir was sequenced in 2017, revealing a specialized photosynthetic apparatus in the light-harvesting complex genes.

• *Pseudotsuga* wood and pollen are recorded in Austria from the Miocene and Pliocene periods.

• The bark can grow to 14 in (36 cm) thick, possibly making the Douglas-fir the most fire-resistant tree native to the Pacific Northwest.

HABITAT AND DISTRIBUTION

Habitat
The Coast Douglas-fir (*Pseudotsuga menziesii var. menziesii*) occurs from near sea level along the coast to 5,900 ft (1,800 m) above sea level. It prefers acidic or neutral soils, and moist, mild climates. The Rocky Mountain Douglas-fir (*Pseudotsuga menziesii var. glauca*) tolerates drier sites, although it can also be found in interior temperate rainforests. Douglas-firs tolerate drier conditions by growing longer taproots.

Distribution
The Coast Douglas-fir (*Pseudotsuga menziesii var. menziesii*) grows in the coastal regions from west-central British Columbia south to central California. In Oregon and Washington, its range is continuous from the eastern edge of the Cascades to the Pacific Ocean. It is found in the Klamath and California Coast Ranges as far south as the Santa Lucia Range. In the Sierra Nevada, it ranges as far south as the Yosemite region. The range of the Rocky Mountain Douglas-fir (*Pseudotsuga menziesii var. glauca*) is north from the Cascades to central British Columbia and southeast to the Mexican border.

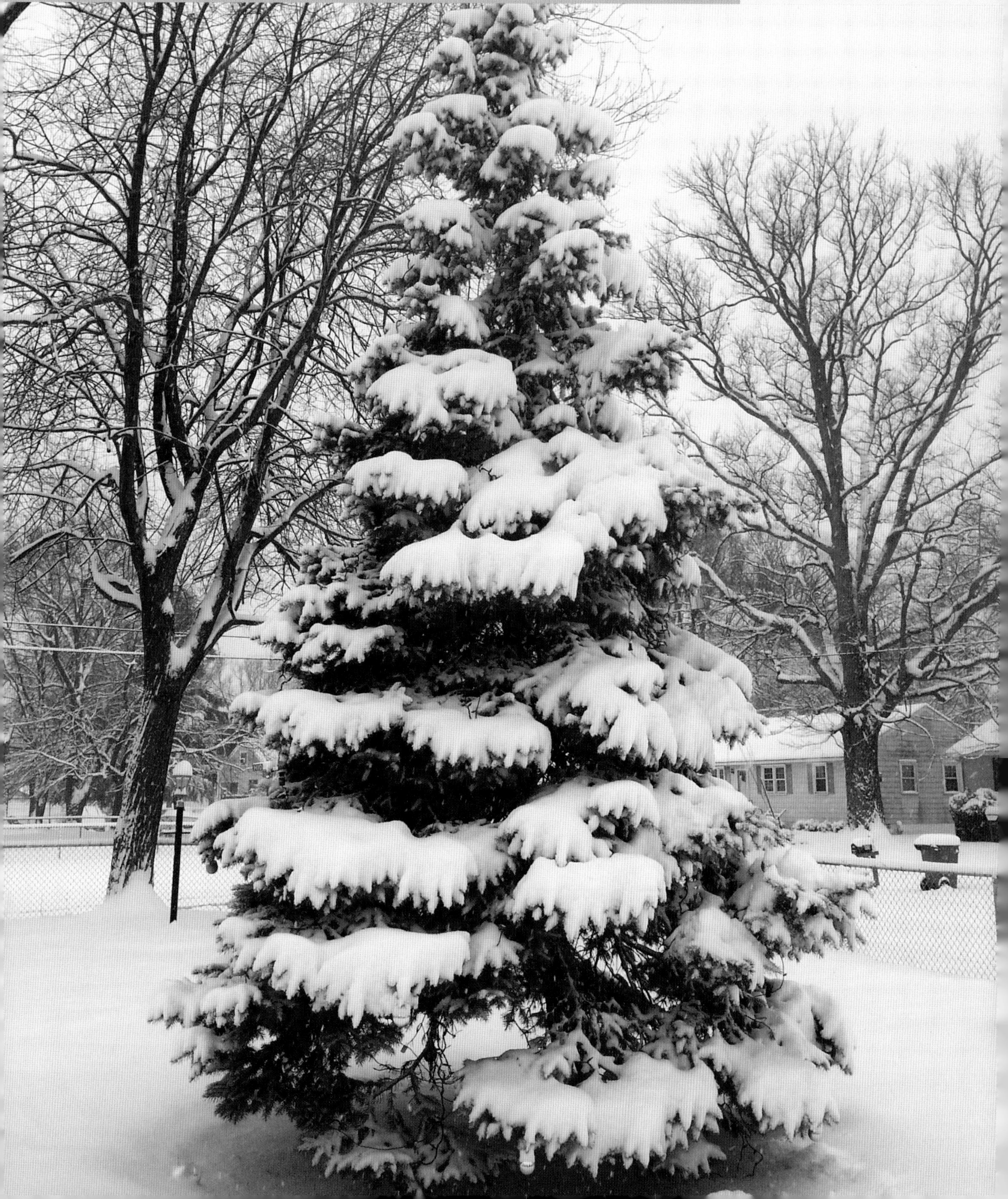

ENGELMANN SPRUCE
Picea engelmannii

Picea engelmannii, commonly known as silver spruce, mountain spruce, white spruce, or Engelmann spruce, is a high-altitude mountain tree. It is native to higher elevations in the Cascade and Rocky Mountains and is the most common spruce found in the Rockies. It is an evergreen tree with a narrowly conic crown when young, which becomes cylindric in older trees. It is well adapted to dealing with deep snows, extreme cold, and harsh winds. The wood is stiff, soft, straight-grained, lightweight, odorless, and easily air-dried, making it an important commercial wood in the U.S. The populations in Mexico, known as the Mexican spruce, *Picea engelmannii* subsp. *mexicana,* are thought by some to belong to a different species.

INTERESTING FACTS

• Trees grown in high altitudes are slow-growing and as such their wood has a specialized use in making instruments such as pianos, violins, harps, and acoustic guitars.

• Outbreaks of spruce beetles have resulted in the destruction of millions of Engelmann spruce trees.

• Engelmann spruce provides excellent hiding and thermal cover for big game including bear, bighorn sheep, moose, elk, and deer. Small animals use spruce trees for roosting sites and protective cover.

Avg height: 82–130 ft (25–40 m)
Avg trunk diameter: 45–59 in (114–150 cm)
Lifespan: 400–600 years

Bark: The bark is scaly and thin, flaking off in circular plates 2–4 in (5–10 cm) across. It is reddish-brown to gray in color and may have a purplish tinge.

Foliage: The leaves are needle-like and rhombic in cross-section. They are .6 - 1.2 in (1.5 - 3 cm) long, glaucous blue-green above and blue-white below.with a wavy margin.

Cones: The cones are slender, cylindrical, and pendulous, 1.6–3.2 in (4–8 cm) in length. They are 0.6 in (1.5 cm) broad when closed, and 1.2 in (3 cm) when open. Their thin, flexible scales have wavy margins and reach 0.6–0.8 in (1.5–2 cm) in length. Cones are dark purple to reddish in color, maturing to pale brown. The seeds are black, 2–3 mm long with a long, slender pale brown wing.

HABITAT AND DISTRIBUTION

Habitat
Picea engelmannii is a high-altitude mountain tree, which grows at elevations between 3,000 and 11,980 ft (900–3,650 m). Rarely, in the northwest of its range, it will grow at lower altitudes.

Distribution
Native to western North America, the Engelmann spruce range extends from southwest Alberta and central British Columbia southwest to northern California and southeast to New Mexico and Arizona. There are two isolated populations in northern Mexico.

VOSS WHITE SPRUCE
Picea glauca

Avg height: 50–100 ft (15–30 m)
Avg trunk diameter: 24–40 in (61–101 cm)
Lifespan: 250–300 years

Bark: The bark is scaly and thin, flaking off in circular plates 2–4 in (5–10 cm) across. The bark is ash-brown or gray-brown and a silvery color when freshly exposed. The bark is mostly less than .3 in (.8 cm) thick and no more than .4 in (.95 cm).by narrow grooves between the plates.

Foliage: Needles are blue-green with sharp tips, reaching .5–.75 in (1.2–2 cm) in length. They have a white waxy coating and a pungent aroma when crushed.

Young cones: The cylindrical and pendulous pale brown cones grow up to 1.2–2.75 in (3–7 cm) long and have flexible scales with smoothly rounded margins. The cones are 0.6 in (1.5 cm) wide when closed and 1 in (2.5 cm) when open. Cones are reddish or green, maturing to pale brown 4–8 months after pollination. Seeds are 2.5–5 mm long with a slender pale brown wing 2–3 mm in length.

White spruce, also known as Porsild spruce, Alberta white spruce, western white spruce, Black Hills spruce, cat spruce, skunk spruce, Canadian spruce, *gaawaandag* and *mina'ig* (Ojibwe), and *épinette blanche* (Canadian French), is a hardy evergreen conifer with a cone-shaped crown. The genus name is derived from the Latin "pix" meaning pitch, which refers to the sticky resin found in the bark of the white spruce. Its specific epithet references the glaucous nature of its needles, which gives them a whitish appearance. In young trees, the crown is narrow-conic, becoming cylindric as the tree ages with slightly drooping branches. In the boreal forests of Canada and Alaska, the white spruce is a climax canopy tree that may grow in soils of glacial origin.

INTERESTING FACTS

• In Canada, the white spruce is of major economic importance, as it is harvested for construction and paper-making, as well as being used as a Christmas tree.

• White spruce is the state tree of South Dakota and the provincial tree of Manitoba.

• The white spruce "big tree" is located in Koochiching County, Minnesota. It stands at 131 ft (40 m) with a trunk diameter of 40 in (101 cm) and a crown spread of 29.5 ft (9 m).

HABITAT AND DISTRIBUTION

Habitat
Picea glauca is commonly found in upland areas and on the margins of lakes and streams. It is native to boreal and northern temperate forests. It grows between sea level and an elevation of 4,990 ft (1,520 m). It can be found in habitats ranging from montane slopes to river banks, bogs, and muskegs.

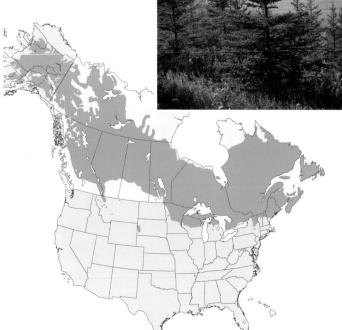

Distribution
The white spruce was native from central Alaska east across southern/central Canada to the Avalon Peninsula in Newfoundland. It has since become naturalized southward into northern border states in the U.S., expanding into New York, Michigan, Wisconsin, Minnesota, Maine, New Hampshire, Vermont, and Montana. There is a disjunct population in the Black Hills of Wyoming and South Dakota.

Avg height: 15–50 ft (5–15 m)
Avg trunk diameter: 6–20 in (15–50 cm)
Lifespan: 250–300 years

Bark: The bark of a young tree is grayish-brown to reddish-brown and thin, often with small, flaky scales. As the tree ages, large and irregularly shaped, thin scales form and the bark darkens in color.

Foliage: The leaves are stiff, four-sided needles that reach 6–15 mm in length. They are dark bluish-green on the upper and paler glaucous green below.and without petals.

Cones: The black spruce has the smallest cones of all spruces. They are spindle-shaped to nearly round, initially dark purple and maturing to red-brown. They are 0.5–1.5 in (1.5–4 cm) long and 0.5–.75 in (1–2 cm) broad and are produced in dense clusters in the upper crown. Once mature, they open to release their seeds but persist on the tree for years.

BLACK SPRUCE
Picea mariana

Picea mariana, commonly known as black spruce, shortleaf black spruce, swamp spruce, bog spruce, *épinette noire* (Canadian French), or *zesegaandag* (Ojibwe), is an abundant, wide-ranging evergreen conifer of the northern parts of North America, particularly Canada. Black spruce is one of the most widely distributed conifers in North America. It is the official tree of the provinces of Labrador and Newfoundland and is the most numerous tree in Labrador. It has a straight trunk with a narrow, pointed crown of drooping branches with upturned tips. The black spruce is an extremely slow grower and its shallow root system makes it susceptible to windthrow. Its growth is most rapid on open sites such as clear-cuts or recent burn areas.

INTERESTING FACTS

• The Latin epithet mariana means "of the Virgin Mary."

• The official "big tree" is in Taylor County, Wisconsin. It stands at 78.75 ft (24 m) with a trunk diameter of 19.7 in (50 cm) and a 19.7 ft (6 m) crown.

• A specimen in Sleeping Giant Provincial Park, Ontario, had a crossdated age of 330 years, making it the oldest known black spruce.

HABITAT AND DISTRIBUTION

Habitat
Picea mariana frequently grows in the biome known as taiga or boreal forest, which is a biome characterized by coniferous forests predominantly consisting of larches, spruces, and pines. The black spruce prefers wetter lowland areas and the site quality affects the tree's growth. It is commonly found in muskegs, swamps, uplands, peat bogs, and transitional sites between uplands and peatlands. Its preferred site is dependant on its location within its range.

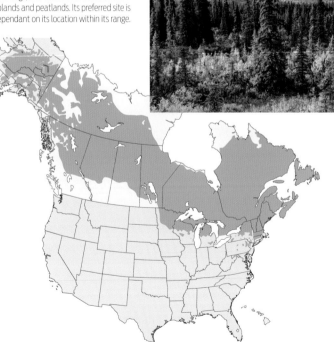

Distribution
The black spruce is widespread across Canada, found in all 3 territories and 10 provinces. The black spruce range extends into northern parts of the United States, in the upper Northeast, the Great Lakes region, and Alaska. Its range is prevented from expanding north by permanently frozen soils, although climate change is favoring its range's northward expansion

Avg height: 59–131 ft (18–40 m)
Avg trunk diameter: 12–24 in (30–60 cm)
Lifespan: 250–450 years

RED SPRUCE
Picea rubens

Picea rubens, known as red spruce, yellow spruce, West Virginia spruce, eastern spruce, *épinette rouge* (Canadian French), and he-balsam, is a spruce native to eastern North America. It is a shade-tolerant, late-successional, perennial coniferous tree with a narrow conical crown. While decidedly conical, the crown is broader than other eastern spruces. Its Latin epithet *rubens* means red, which may refer either to the cones or the bark. In the Great Smoky Mountains National Park, extensive virgin spruce-fir forests are preserved. The wood of the red spruce is light in weight and color, resilient, and straight-grained.

Bark: The bark is gray-brown to reddish-brown and is thin and scaly. The interior of the bark is a red-brown color.

INTERESTING FACTS

• Red spruce is often used to make higher-end violins and acoustic guitars, as well as soundboards and organ pipes, as it is an excellent tonewood.

• The red spruce is the provincial tree of Nova Scotia.

• The tallest known specimen and the official "big tree" are both located within the Great Smoky Mountains National Park. The tallest known tree is 152 ft (46.33 m) and the "big tree" is 146.7 ft (44.7 m) tall with a trunk diameter of 48.5 in (123 cm) and a 24 ft (7.3 m) crown.

Foliage: The leaves are yellow-green and needlelike, reaching 0.45–0.6 in (1.2–1.5 cm) in length. They are curved and four-sided, coming to a sharp point. The needles extend from all sides of the twig.

HABITAT AND DISTRIBUTION

Habitat
The red spruce is often found in pure stands or mixed forests with black spruce, balsam fir, or eastern white pine. It prefers well-drained but moist sandy loam, usually at high altitudes. Red spruce grows best in a moist, cool climate and attains maximum development in the higher elevations of the southern Appalachian Mountains where the rainfall is heavier during the growing season and the atmosphere is more humid than in other parts of its range.

Cones: Cones are cylindrical and a glossy red-brown color, reaching 1.25–2 in (3–5 cm) in length. The mature cones are brown, have stiff, fan-shaped scales, and hang down from branches.

Distribution
The red spruce ranges from Nova Scotia and eastern Quebec, west to the Adirondack Mountains and south along the Appalachians through New England to western North Carolina. In the southern Appalachian spruce-fir forest, a distinct ecosystem only found in the highest elevations of the Southern Appalachian Mountains, the red spruce is one of two primary tree types.

SITKA SPRUCE
Picea sitchensis

Avg height: 125–180 ft (38–55 m)
Avg trunk diameter: 36–60 in (91.5–152.5 cm)
Lifespan: 700–800 years

Bark: The bark is scaly and thin, flaking off in small, circular plates 2–8 in (5–20 cm) across. As it grows in cool, wet climates, its thin bark is not adapted to resist fire damage and is very susceptible.

Foliage: The leaves are sharp, stiff, and needlelike, flattened in cross-section and up to 0.6–1 in (1.5–2.5 cm) in length. They are dark blue-green above and blue-white below.

Cones: The cones are slender cylindrical and pendulous, reaching 2.5–4 in (6–10 cm) in length. They are 0.75 in (2 cm) wide when closed and 1.25 in (3 cm) wide when open. The scales are long and flexible, reaching 0.625–0.75 in (1.5–2 cm), and the bracts above the scales are longer than those of any other spruce. The seeds are 3 mm long with a long, slender, pale brown wing and hang down from branches.

The Sitka spruce is a coniferous, evergreen tree. It is the largest species of spruce by far and the world's fifth-largest conifer, behind the western red cedar, kauri, coast redwood, and giant sequoia. It is also the third-tallest conifer species after coast Douglas fir and coast redwood. When young, the tree has a broad conic crown, which becomes cylindrical as the tree ages. On older trees, the trunk may be bare of branches for up to 98–131 ft (30–40 m). The Sitka spruce provides important habitat for a wide range of amphibians, reptiles, birds, and mammals. In British Columbia and Alaska, the needles make up nearly 90% of the winter diet of blue grouse.

INTERESTING FACTS

• The Sitka spruce is one of the few documented species to exceed 300 ft (90 m) in height, with specimens standing in Carmanah Walbran Provincial Park, Pacific Rim National Park, Olympic National Park, and Prairie Creek Redwoods State Park.

• The wood of the Sitka spruce is widely used in the manufacturing of guitars, harps, violins, and pianos, because its regular, knot-free rings and high strength-to-weight ratio makes it an excellent sound conductor.

• Many aircraft made before World War II were made out of Sitka spruce wood, including the Wright brothers' Flyer.

HABITAT AND DISTRIBUTION

Habitat
The Sitka spruce is associated with temperate rainforests and prefers soils with high levels of phosphorus, calcium, and magnesium, and is tolerant to salty spray that is common in a coastal dune habitat. It prefers full sun and is a pioneer species on deglaciated terrain, uplifted beaches, sand dunes, and landslides. In coastal forests, it is a climax species.

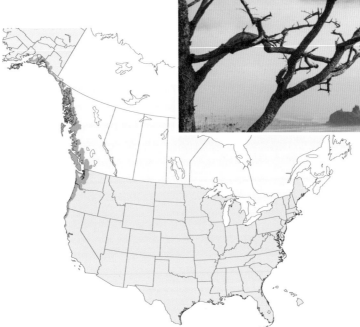

Distribution
The Sitka spruce is prevalent in southeast Alaska. Its range extends along the western coast of Canada and the U.S., reaching into northernmost California. Its northwestern limit is on Kenai Peninsula, Alaska, and its southeasternmost limit is near Fort Bragg, California. It is found within a few miles of the coast in the southern portion of its range. While it extends inland along river floodplains north of Oregon, it does not extend more than 50 miles (80 km) from the Pacific Ocean at any point.

TAMARACK
Larix laricin

Avg height: 32–64 ft (10–20 m)
Avg trunk diameter: 12–23.5 in (30–60 cm)
Lifespan: 300–500 years

Bark: The bark is thick and scaly. It is dark in color with a scarlet tint just visible between the scales of the bark.

Foliage: The leaves are needlelike and reach 0.8–1.2 in (2–3 cm) in length. They are a blue-green color and turn a bright showy yellow in fall before falling, leaving pale pinkish-brown shoots bare until spring.

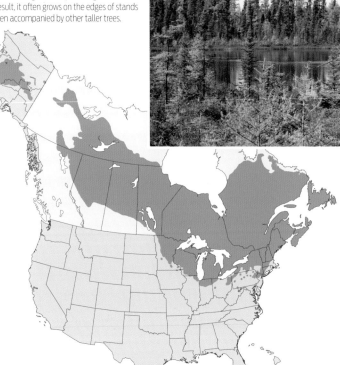

Cones: The cones are the tiniest of any larch, measuring just 0.4–1.2 in (1–3 cm) long. Each cone contains only 12–25 scales, each containing a seed. When young, they are a brilliant maroon and resemble tiny roses, but dull to brown as they mature. Seeds are produced 4–6 months after pollination.

Larix laricina, commonly known as tamarack, tamarack larch, Canadian larch, American larch, eastern larch, black larch, red larch, eastern tamarack, kackmatack, and mézèle allicin, is an arboreal *Pinaceae* species. The name tamarack is from the Native American Algonquian language because this tribe discovered and named the tree. As it is a typical early invasive species, tamarack is often the first to develop after an area is disturbed and establish dominance over an area. The tamarack is remarkably tolerant of cold and can grow in the Arctic in temperatures as low as -85 ºF (-65 ºC) by establishing tree lines along the edge of the tundra; however, it does not grow as tall in particularly cold temperatures, many not exceeding 5 feet (1.5 m) in height.

INTERESTING FACTS

• The wood of the tamarack is strong and durable but is also flexible in thin strips. It was used by the Algonquian people to make snowshoes and other items where both strength and flexibility were required.

• Tamarack is an iconic tree of the Northwest Territories of Canada and is mentioned in "The Battler" from Ernest Hemingway's collection of short stories In Our Time.

• It is the northernmost tree in North America as it occupies the arctic treeline.

HABITAT AND DISTRIBUTION

Habitat
The tamarack is extremely cold-hardy, tolerating temperatures down to -85 ºF (-65 ºC). While it grows best in marshes, it may also be found on dry, sandy soil. It is sensitive to light levels, preferring full sun. As a result, it often grows on the edges of stands when accompanied by other taller trees.

Distribution
Larix laricina can be found from the Northwest Territories and eastern Yukon, east to Newfoundland. It also stands to the south in northeastern Minnesota to the Carnesvill Swamps of West Virginia and northeast to Maine. Disjunct populations grow in central Alaska.

WESTERN LARCH
Larix occidentalis

Larix occidentalis, also known as western larch or western American larch, is an arboreal *Pinaceae* species endemic to the highlands of western North America. There are three species of North American larches: western, eastern (*Larix laricin*, tamarack), and subalpine (*Larix lyallii*), which is native to northwestern North America . These trees are fast-growing hardwoods and graft easily, therefore more often growing vegetatively than germination from seed. The seeds are an important winter food source for some birds, including the redpoll, the white-winged crossbill, and the pine siskin. They have a narrow conic crown with level to upswept main branches and drooping side branches.

Avg height: 98–197 (30–60 m)
Avg trunk diameter: 39–59 in (100–150 cm)
Lifespan: 500–1,000 years

Bark: The bark is gray or brown to reddish-orange in color. The bark is thick and furling, becoming cracked and furrowed into jigsaw-shaped platelets as the tree ages.

Foliage: The needles are light green and extremely thin, reaching 0.8–2 in (2–5 cm) long. In the fall, they turn a bright yellow before falling.

Cones: Male cones are small and yellowish-orange in color. Female seed cones are ovoid-cylindric, reaching 0.5–2 in (2–5 cm) in length, with each cone holding 40–80 seed scales. When young, the cones are reddish-purple, darkening to brown as the scales open to release the seeds 4–6 months after pollination. Open cones persist on the tree for years, turning gray-black.

INTERESTING FACTS

• Native American tribes drank an infusion of young shoots to treat laryngitis and tuberculosis.

• The western larch is used in the production of Venice turpentine, which is a specialized solvent and a source of material for organic syntheses.

• The thick bark and high limbs make the western larch the most fire-resistant tree in the Pacific Northwest.

• The largest known specimen stands at Seeley Lake, Montana and is 153 ft (4 m) tall with a circumference of 22 ft (6. m) and a 34 ft (10 m) crown.

HABITAT AND DISTRIBUTION

Habitat
These trees are very cold tolerant, able to survive temperatures as low as -58 ºF (-50 ºC). They cannot tolerate waterlogged soils, requiring soils with good drainage. They grow at elevations between 1,600–7,900 ft (500–2,400 m).

Distribution
The western larch is found in the mountains of western North America, including southeastern British Columbia and southern Alberta in Canada; and eastern Washington, eastern Oregon, northern Idaho, and western Montana in the U.S.

PINE LEAVES

Within the pine family, the pine genus, *Pinus*, is divided into two subgenera: *Pinus*, known as the hard pines, and *Strobus*, the soft pines. Most of the *Strobus* subgenus in North America are white pines, distinguished by needles that are clustered in groups of five growing out of each fascicle on the branch, while most of the *Pinus* subgenus, with the exception of the Red Pine, have needles that are grouped in threes. How these clusters are spaced on the twigs can result in great variety, even among closely related species. The Pinyon, also in the *Strobus* subgenus, has one or two needles in each fascicle. Larches (*Larix*), unlike pines, are deciduous—they lose their leaves in winter. Their needle-shaped leaves grow in bundles of 10–20 in each fascicle.

Red Pine *Pinus resinosa*
Pinus

Lodgepole Pine *Pinus contorta*
Pinus

Shortleaf Pine *Pinus echinata*
Pinus

Ponderosa Pine *Pinus ponderosa*
Pinus

Table Mountain Pine *Pinus pungens*
Pinus

Pitch Pine *Pinus rigida*
Pinus

Pinyon *Pinus edulis*
Strobus/Parrya

Limber Pine *Pinus flexilis*
Strobus

Sugar Pine *Pinus lambertiana*
Strobus

Slash Pine *Pinus elliottii*
Pinus

Spruce Pine *Pinus glabra*
Pinus

Jeffrey Pine *Pinus jeffreyi*
Pinus

Longleaf Pine *Pinus palustris*
Pinus

Pond Pine *Pinus serotina*
Pinus

Loblolly Pine *Pinus taeda*
Pinus

Virginia Pine *Pinus virginiana*
Pinus

Western White Pine *Pinus monticola*
Strobus

Eastern White Pine *Pinus strobus*
Strobus

Tamarack *Larix laricina*

Western Larch *Larix occidentalis*

Avg height: 50–100 ft (15.25–30.5 m)
Avg trunk diameter : 8–24 in (20–61 cm)
Lifespan: 150–400 years

Bark: The bark of the lodgepole pine is orangey-brown to gray in color and thin, which minimizes the tree's defense against fire. The texture is finely scaled.and peels in narrow, longitudinal strips.

Needles: Needles are twisted in a spiral and come to sharp points. They grow in fascicles of two and are a dark green color. They typically reach 1.6–3 in (4–8 cm) in length and grow alternate on their twigs.

Cones: Female cones are tipped with sharp, spiny scales, reaching 1–3 in (3–7 cm) in length, and often require exposure to high temperatures (such as forest fires) to open and release their seeds. Seed cones vary in shape from egg-shaped to cylindrical and reach 8–1.6 in (2–4 cm) in length.

LODGEPOLE PINE
Pinus contorta

Pinus contorta, commonly known as lodgepole pine, tamarack pine, or black pine, is a common evergreen species in western North America. The common name by which this species of pine is known in North America, lodgepole, is due to the use of its lumber in the construction of Native American lodges, a form of tent or tipi made by covering 15 to 18 *Pinus contorta* trunks with animal skins. The trunks of this species are long, straight, and light, which made it ideal for transport on horseback in nomadic buffalo hunting cultures. The tribes traveled long distances across the plains to look for the pines that grew only in the mountainous areas.

INTERESTING FACTS

• Different parts of the plant were used by indigenous peoples of California and the Pacific Northwest to treat a number of ailments.

• As the wood of the lodgepole pine is uniform in texture, straight grained, and light, it is suitable for paneling, plywood, and lumber.

• Older lodgepole pines are susceptible to mountain pine beetles, which lay their eggs under the bark.

HABITAT AND DISTRIBUTION

Habitat
It's a widespread tree along the coast and in dry upland to subalpine forests in western North America, but it's uncommon in lowland rainforests. It may thrive in a variety of soil types, but favors those with adequate drainage.

Distribution
The lodgepole pine is one of the most widely distributed tree species in western North America. Its region extends from Alaska south to Mexico and east to South Dakota, and it is found in Colorado, Idaho, Montana, Oregon, Utah, Washington, and Wyoming.

Avg height: 80–125 ft (25–40 m)
Avg trunk diameter: 24–36 in (61–91 cm)
Lifespan: 120–200 years

Bark: The bark is thick and tends to have a reddish-brown to almost black color. It is broken into large, irregular, and scaly plates. The thick bark protects the tree and dormant buds from fire, turning it into a relatively fire-resistant species and preventing basal injury, which is relatively uncommon.

Needles: The leaves of the shortleaf pine are needles, which grow in bundles of 2 and occasionally 3. The needles tend to be 3–5 in (7.6–12.7 cm) long and grow straight and sharp, without twisting. Flexible and thin, they have a dark green color that can sometimes take a blue tint.

Cones: Male and female cones often grow in the same tree, the former being pale purple in color and the latter a pale pink. Male cones can usually be recognized as they grow in clusters at the tip of twigs. The ovoid, short-stalked cones are usually not produced until the tree reaches 20 years of age. Once emptied the cones stay attached to the tree for years.

SHORTLEAF PINE
Pinus echinata

Pinus echinata, commonly known as the shortleaf pine, is an evergreen tree that is Missouri's only native pine. It was once a dominant species in the Ozarks but its population was decimated by extensive logging between 1890 and 1920, after which oaks spread into what used to be pinelands. In recent years, efforts have been made to restore the numbers of this once dominant species. The shortleaf pine is the most widely distributed of the southern yellow pines and features a straight trunk and an open crown. The species is particularly important for the lumber industry, as it is used for construction and millworks, among a wide variety of other uses. Seedlings sprout after fire damage or after sustaining an injury.

INTERESTING FACTS

• The shortleaf pine has a medium-thick bark that can protect the dormant buds. The species is also considered fire-resistant and regenerates well after being affected by fire.

• Shortleaf pine forests were key for the growth of railroads, playing a vital role in America's economy.

• Arkansas contains more shortleaf pines than any other state in the country, and it was named the state tree in 1939 in recognition of the state's pine timber resources and reforestation efforts.

HABITAT AND DISTRIBUTION

Habitat
Pinus echinata grows in upland forests, both moist and dry, as well as in the margins of glades, preferring acidic soils. This pine grows best on well-drained deep soils, particularly silty or sandy loam, which tend to be characteristic of the Gulf Coast and the South Atlantic region.

Distribution
The shortleaf pine grows on the widest geographic range of all pine species in the southeastern region of the U.S. Its natural range extends from southeastern New York to northern Florida, as well as throughout the Gulf States. Inland, *Pinus echinata* can be found in western Pennsylvania, southern Ohio, southern Illinois and eastern Texas, as well as in southern Missouri and eastern Oklahoma.

Avg height: 10–20 ft (3–6 m)
Avg trunk diameter: 20–40 in
(50.8–101.6 cm)
Lifespan: 500–1,000 years

Bark: The bark of *Pinus edulis* tends to be gray to pale or dark brown or pale reddish-brown. On rare occasions, the bark can be nearly back. It has small rough scales and an irregularly furrowed texture. The bark is very thin and covers the trunk, which tends to be crooked or twisted.

Needles: Needles are slightly thicker than most other pine needles and pointed. They Easily distinguished by their yellow-green color and slightly curved shape, they grow in bundles of two or occasionally three. They can reach 2 in (5 cm) long and remain on the tree for up to nine years.

Cones: As a slow-growing tree, *Pinus edulis* can take up to 100 years to start producing cones. The cones have a rounded shape, are usually 1–2 in (2.5–5 cm) long, and tend to have fewer scales than other pine trees. They open into a rosette with large and thick scales. The edible seeds have thin brown shells and measure about .5 in (1.25 cm).

PINYON
Pinus edulis

Pinus edulis, commonly known as pinyon or sometimes piñon, is a picturesque small to medium-sized evergreen pine often recognizable for its gnarled figure. Its edible seeds, known as pinyon nuts, pine nuts, or piñones in Spanish, are a very popular commercial wild nut crop. Once a staple in the food of Native American tribes in the Southwest, today they are consumed all over the world whether raw, roasted, or even caramelized. The pinyon descends from a member of the Madro Tertiary Geoflora, a group of drought-resistant trees native to North America. It is a small to medium-sized tree, which can be identified due to its numerous branches, thick trunk, and rounded crown. It is considered a very slow-growing, long-living tree.

INTERESTING FACTS

• 22% of forests in Colorado are pinyon forests, making it the state's dominant species.

• The pinyon at the highest elevation ever recorded is in the Kaibab National Forest of northern Arizona, at 10,400 ft (3,170 m) above sea level.

• The highly nutritious content of pine nuts is key for the tree's survival: in arid settings, where it grows, the seeds will not germinate if dropped on the ground.

• Pinyon jays—named for the tree—as well as wild turkeys, bears, and other wildlife bury the nuts for future use, which helps them sprout and grow.

HABITAT AND DISTRIBUTION

Habitat
Pinus edulis grows best at a moderate altitude, ranging from 5,200–7,900 ft (1,600–2,400 m) above sea level. On very rare occasions, they can be found as low as 4,600 ft (1,400 m) or as high as 9,900 ft (3,000 m). They tend to grow on arid open woodlands, where they mix with junipers to create a biome or plant community known as a pinyon-juniper woodland.

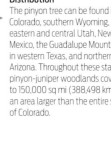

Distribution
The pinyon tree can be found in Colorado, southern Wyoming, eastern and central Utah, New Mexico, the Guadalupe Mountains in western Texas, and northern Arizona. Throughout these states, pinyon-juniper woodlands cover up to 150,000 sq mi (388,498 km²), an area larger than the entire state of Colorado.

Avg height: 59–98 ft (18–30 m)
Avg trunk diameter: 24–30 in (61–76 cm)
Lifespan: 150–200 years

SLASH PINE
Pinus elliottii

Pinus elliotii, commonly known as slash pine, is a conifer tree that grows in the southeastern U.S. It gets its common name from its habitat: the swampy ground where it grows, known as "slashes." Other common names include swamp pine or yellow slash pine. The slash pine is very fast-growing, but for the same reason tends to be rather short-lived, at least by pine standards, usually not surpassing 200 years. This species requires moist soils to grow well and is common along swamps, bays, and hammocks of the Florida Everglades. Although its native range is quite small, it has widened its distribution in the last few decades due to improved fire control in the south, a management strategy that was used by Native Americans but fell out of favor until the 1950s and 1960s.

INTERESTING FACTS

• For a pine species the slash pine is unusually strong. Its wood is stronger than most hardwoods and can even be compared to some types of ironwoods, having a greater strength-to-weight ratio.

• In the late 1950s, fusiform rust led to a massive tree death that affected slash pines. The parasite that causes it affects mostly young trees in newly planted areas, therefore decimating the still-new populations of pines planted for the pine industry.

• *Pinus elliottii* is particularly vulnerable to fire when young. Improved fire protection has allowed it to spread to drier sites, not usually considered its preferred habitat.

Bark: The trunk of the slash pine is usually straight, and the bark tends to be a red-brown color. When young, it has a furrowed texture, which then becomes platy. The surface of the plates is covered in loose scales that flake off to reveal a light brown to cinnamon color underneath. Its thick bark and open crown allow it to survive fires.

Needles: The needles are very slender and flexible and grow in clusters of three or sometimes two per fascicle. They are usually 7–9 in (17.75–22.8 cm) long. It can be distinguished from longleaf pines by its shorter and slender needles. They are usually dark green in color.

Cones: *Pinus elliotti* has glossy red-brown cones, that can be between 2–6 in (5–15 cm) long. The scales end in thick prickles. It may be distinguished from loblolly pine by its larger red-brown cones. Trees usually begin producing cones between 10 and 15 years of age.

HABITAT AND DISTRIBUTION

Habitat
The slash pine grows in wet flatwoods and sandy subtropical maritime forests. It tends to favor warm and humid areas and can be limited by factors such as competition with other species or fire. While it can adapt to a variety of soils, *Pinus elliottii* tends to grow best close to bodies of water, both thanks to the moisture levels of the soil and the fire protection it offers. Grows well on acidic soils in full sun or even partial shade.

Distribution
Slash pine forests are mostly found in Florida and Georgia, extending from South Carolina west to southeastern Louisiana and south to the Florida Keys. Although not native to the state, it is also common in east Texas, where it was introduced in 1926. *Pinus elliotti* has the smallest native range of the four major southern American pines..

LIMBER PINE
Pinus flexilis

Avg height: 40–50 ft (12–15 m)
Avg trunk diameter: 24–36 in (61–91 cm)
Lifespan: 800–1,000 years

Bark: *Pinus flexilis* has a heavily creased, dark grayish-brown bark, which protects a lightweight and soft wood. The bark is smooth on the younger branches and becomes platy and scaly on older and larger ones. When young, the bark of the limber pine tends to be a light gray color.

Needles: The long needles of the limber pine have a dark, blueish-green color. The limber pine can often be distinguished by the fact that its needles grow in bundles of 5. The only other pine species that shares this characteristic is the whitebark pine, which can sometimes make it difficult to tell the two apart.

Cones: During the growing season, limber pine cones can be recognized for their green color and oblong shape. At other times, limber pine can be distinguished from the whitebark pine tree by the fact that old cones tend to be lying on the ground underneath it. Its pollen cones are pale red or yellow and mature 2 years after pollination.

Pinus flexilis, commonly known as limber pine or Rocky Mountain white pine, is a species of pine tree that grows in the mountains of Mexico, Canada, and the western United States. It receives its "limber" common name thanks to its pliant and flexible branches and can be recognized by its dark, blueish-green long needles. The limber pine is typically a high-elevation pine, although it can grow in a wide range of altitudes. Limber pines live extremely long lives: the oldest living specimen is thought to be almost 3,000 years old. Like all in the white pine, or *Strobus*, subgenus of *Pinus*, its needles grow out of the fascicles in bundles of five, and its cones are relatively longer than those of the *Pinus* subgenus.

INTERESTING FACTS

• The oldest limber pine found, in Eagle Cap Wilderness, Oregon, was 2,000 years old. Another, found in Utah and known as "Twister," was confirmed to be at least 1,700 years old. One of the oldest living limber pines grows on the banks of North Saskatchewan River in Alberta. It is believed to be close to 3,000 years old.

• The height of the limber pine depends on growing conditions. Its average height ranges between 40–50 ft (12–15 m), but in the windswept Rocky Mountains it becomes unusually stunted, growing to less than 10 ft (3 m) in height.

• In the 1800s the limber pine was regularly used for mine props and railroad ties, but has little commercial value today.

HABITAT AND DISTRIBUTION

Habitat
Typically a high elevation pine, *Pinus flexilis is* found in a wide range of altitudes, from 2,790 up to 12,500 ft (850–3,810 m), depending on the latitude. In the northern part of its natural range, it can be found in the montane zone, while in the middle of its range it is often found in windswept subalpine zones. In the southernmost part of its range is can be found in the subalpine zone. It tends to favor calcareous soils.

Distribution
Its natural range covers the mountains of Mexico, Canada, and the western U.S. Most limber pines can be found in the Rocky Mountains, in a range covering extending from southwestern Alberta and southeastern British Columbia south through Colorado and New Mexico, and well into northern states of Mexico. It is also found in Nevada and Utah, as well as in northern California.

SPRUCE PINE
Pinus glabra

Avg height: 79–110 ft (24 - 33.5 m)
Avg Trunk Diameter: 22–44 in (61–122 cm)
Lifespan: 80–115 years

Bark: Mature bark is gray and fissured in long plates, while younger bark is smooth and gray.

Needles: Two straight needles per fascicle and last on the tree for 2 to 3 years, averaging 1.6–3.2 in (4–8 cm) in length and 0.7–1.2 mm in width.

Cones: Pollen cones are long and cylindrical, 4–6 in (10–15 cm) in length and purple-brown. Seed cones are red-brown aging to gray, long ovoid before opening and ovoid-cylindrical when open, and 1.5–2.75 in (3.3–7 cm) long. Seeds are shed soon after maturing at 2 years.

Pinus glabra, also commonly known as spruce pine, cedar pine, or Walter pine, grows in a wide band across the Southeast between the Atlantic and Gulf Coasts. It is an evergreen coniferous species of tree that grows straight although often slightly bent or twisted with whorled branches spreading and ascending to a pyramidal or rounded crown. The twigs are slender and purple-red to red-brown to start, eventually aging to gray, with a smooth surface. In contrast with other species of pines, the spruce pine differs from other pines in that it is typically found in forests of mixed hardwood trees, while most pines grow in largely pure pine forests. In order to grow in mixed habitats and compete successfully with other tree species, the spruce pine has adapted to greater shade tolerance than most other pines.

INTERESTING FACTS

• When used in lumber manufacturing, the spruce pine must be dried separately from other southern pine species due to its radically different drying rates.

• The scientific name *Pinus glabra*, given in 1788 by Thomas Walter, refers to the tree's waxy, smooth shoots and branchlets.

• The known tallest spruce pine is found in the Moody Tract Natural Area in Georgia, standing at 116.9 ft (35.63 m).

• During the winter, these trees are heavily utilized by turkeys for roosting as they are often the only cover in the area.

HABITAT AND DISTRIBUTION

Habitat
Spruce pine grows in a climate characterized by long, hot, humid summers and mild winters with evenly distributed annual rainfall, averaging 50 in (1,270 mm) and as such has a low drought tolerance. These pines are found in wet bottomlands and therefore rarely experience fire and are not well adapted to it. Their thin bark is easily damaged and, unlike some other pines, seedling establishment is not enhanced by fire disturbances.

Distribution
The spruce pine grows in a wide band across the Southeast, found in low coastal areas in Louisiana, Mississippi, Alabama, Florida, Georgia, and South Carolina in mixed-hardwood forests. Found from sea level to elevations of 500 ft (150 m) in the sandy alluvium and mesic woodland of the Gulf and Atlantic coastal plains. The cold hardiness limit is between 10° and 20°F (-12.1° and -6.7°C).

Avg height: 170–200 ft (51.8–60.9 m)
Avg trunk diameter: 3 ft (1 m)
Lifespan: 400–500 years

Bark: Yellow-brown in color, turning cinnamon-brown as it matures. Bark becomes grooved with loose, scaly plates separated by deep fissures over time.

Needles: Needles are twisted and fairly stiff. They are a gray-blue color and grow in bundles of three, reaching 4.7–11 in (12–28 cm) in length, and persist 5–8 years on the tree.

Cones: Hanging, pointed cones reach 4.7–10.2 in (12–26 cm) in length and vary between long and conical or egg-shaped. Once fully mature, reddish-brown cones fall off to spread seeds; large cone drops occur in 2–4 year intervals.

JEFFREY PINE
Pinus jeffreyi

Pinus jeffreyi, named after its botanist documenter John Jeffrey, is also known as Jeffrey pine, Jeffrey's pine, yellow pine, and black pine. Mainly found in California, it also grows in western Nevada, southwestern Oregon, and northern Baja California in Mexico. The crowns are semiclosed and conical, flattening out when mature. Its branches grow horizontally and its twigs are orange-brown to green in color, maturing to a dark brown and black. The Jeffrey pine is often the dominant species in areas of very dry or serpentine soils, although in more productive and mixed-conifer forests, the tree's dominance is dependent on recurrent fires that create gaps in the canopy. While the tree typically grows straight, the pine can be deformed by high winds at high-elevation sites, leaving the tree bent as it grows.

INTERESTING FACTS

• *Pinus jeffreyi* is closely related to the ponderosa pine (*Pinus ponderosa*) and is similar in appearance, with the main distinguishing feature being their cones. The Jeffrey pine cones have scale barbs that point inward while the ponderosa pine cone scale barbs point outward; this leads to the memory device for distinguishing between the two trees: "gentle Jeffrey and prickly ponderosa."

• The largest *Pinus jeffreyi* (by trunk volume) is the Eureka Valley Giant, which stands in the Stanislaus National Forest in Northern California.

• The bark has a distinctive, pleasant fragrance described as butterscotch, apple, violet, vanilla, lemon, or pineapple.

HABITAT AND DISTRIBUTION

Habitat
While both *Pinus jeffreyi* and *Pinus ponderosa* are high-altitude species, the former is more stress tolerant. In drier and colder climates, on poorer soils, and at higher elevations, *Pinus jeffreyi* is the dominant tree. It is a highly adaptable tree and is suited to a wide range of soils, including sandy and clay loams.

Distribution
Pinus jeffreyi grows from southwest Oregon through much of California on the eastern side of the Sierra Nevada to northern Baja California in Mexico. It grows widely at 4,900–6,900 ft (1,500–2,100 m) altitude in the north of its range and at 5,900–9,500 ft (1,800–2,900 m) in the south. *Pinus jeffreyi* has a cold hardiness limit between 10° and 20°F (-12.1° and -6.7°C).

SUGAR PINE
Pinus lambertiana

Avg height: 100–200 ft (30–60 m)
Avg trunk diameter: 3–10 ft (1–3 m)
Lifespan: 400–500 years

Bark: Color ranges from cinnamon to gray-brown and is deeply furrowed with long, scaly plates.

Needles: Like other members of the white pine group, the sugar pine has needles that grow 5 per fascicle, spreading to ascending. The thin, sharp, straight needles persist 2–4 years and reach 2–4 in (5–10 cm) in length.

Cones: The longest of all conifer cones, ranging from 7.75–19.75 in (20–50 cm), and reaching an exceptional 31.5 in (80 cm) long. The cones contain seeds that are 0.5–0.75 in (1–2 cm) with 0.75–1.25 in (2–3 cm) long wings that aid their dispersal by wind.

The sugar pine (*Pinus lambertiana*) is the tallest and largest of all pines and was called "the most princely of the genus" by its discoverer David Douglas. Naturalist John Muir called the sugar pine the "king of the conifers." While the pines grow at a wide range of elevations, some of the tallest specimens have been found at surprisingly low elevations where they must tolerate intense summer heat and frequent fires. The sugar pine is a member of the white pine group and, like all members of that group, has needles that grow in bundles of five. *Pinus lambertiana* is known for having the longest cones of any conifer, reaching an exceptional 31.5 in (80 cm) in length. The common name comes from the tree's sweet resin, which was used as a sweetener by Native Americans.

INTERESTING FACTS

• The tallest recorded specimen can be found in Yosemite National Park and is 273.75 ft (83.45 m) tall. The second tallest recorded was called the "Yosemite Giant," a 269.2 ft (82 m) tall tree in Yosemite National Park, which died in 2007 from a bark beetle attack.

• Native Americans ate the sweetish seeds and sap while the odorless wood is a preferred method for packing fruit and its straight grain makes it a useful material for crafting organ pipes.

• A wide range of wildlife species rely on the sugar pine seeds due to their large size and high nutritional value, including yellow pine chipmunks, Steller's jays, and black bears.

HABITAT AND DISTRIBUTION

Habitat
While sugar pine naturally grows over a wide range of soil conditions, with its best development reached on mesic soils of medium textures. As the native range of the sugar pine is extensive, the temperature and precipitation widely varies throughout its growing range, as does elevation. Much of the terrain that contains sugar pine is rugged and steep and the pines grow best as elevation increases, with optimal growth occurring at middle elevation. Sugar pine always grows in a mixed forest and as such is shade tolerant in youth before it crests the cover of the surrounding trees.

Distribution
Pinus lambertiana extends from the western slope of the Cascade Range in north central Oregon to the Sierra San Pedro Martir in Baja California, Mexico. Over 80% of the growing stock is in California, where the most dense populations are found on the west slope of the Sierra Nevada in mixed conifer forests.

Avg height: 100–200 ft (30–60 m)
Avg Trunk Diameter: 36–96 in (91–244 cm)
Lifespan: 300–400 years

Bark: Thin, gray, and smooth when young. Bark becomes furrowed into distinctive scaly hexagonal and rectangular plates as the tree matures.

Needles: Straight or slightly twisted blue-green needles grow in fascicles of 5, spreading to ascending. They persist 3–4 years on the branch and reach 1.6–4 in (4–10 cm) and 1 mm wide.

Cones: Pollen cones are 0.4–0.6 in (1–1.5 cm) long, ellipsoid shaped, and yellow-green in color. Seed cones reach 4–5 in (10–25 cm) in length and are creamy brown to yellow in color, growing in clusters.

WESTERN WHITE PINE
Pinus monticola

Pinus monticola, also called California mountain pine, soft pine, finger cone pine, mountain pine, little sugar pine, or silver pine, is a species that occurs in the northern Rocky Mountains, the Coast Range, the Cascade Range, and the Sierra Nevada. Extending into Canada, the western white pine is also found in California, Oregon, Nevada, Idaho, Montana, and Washington. It is the most prevalent five-needled pine of western North America. Its branches are spreading-ascending and whorled, and its slender twigs are a pale red-brown when young, changing to a smooth purple-brown or gray as the tree matures. Because it is greatly affected by the western white pine blister rust (*Cronartium ribicola*), efforts have been made to promote the growth of variants that are more resistant to the fungi. In the absence of the rust, the species commonly reaches 300–400 years old.

INTERESTING FACTS

• Western white pine is the state tree of Idaho and is sometimes referred to as the Idaho pine.

• Used as an important timber tree, the species yields high-quality, straight-grained wood of good strength and dimensions and is commonly used for interior construction and paneling, as well as matches, tooth picks, and furniture.

• Native Americans wove baskets from the bark, collected the cambium in the spring for food, concocted a poultice for dressing wounds from the pitch, and chewed the resin.

HABITAT AND DISTRIBUTION

Habitat
This species' natural habitat is in moist mountain soils or lowland fog forests, and occasionally forested bogs. Western white pines are often found in mixed conifer forests and occasionally in pure stands.

Distribution
Pinus monticola is found from British Columbia south into western Montana, Idaho, and Washington down to California. It grows at a variety of elevations that reaches down to sea level in areas, particularly in Washington and Oregon, and up to 6,000–10,000 ft (1,828–3,048 m) on the western face of the Sierra Nevada. This tree has a cold hardiness limit between -30º and -20ºF (-34.3º and -38.9ºC).

LONGLEAF PINE
Pinus palustris

Avg height: 60–120 ft (18.2–36.6 m)
Avg trunk diameter: 28–48 in (71–122 cm)
Lifespan: 300 years

Bark: As the tree matures, the bark forms flaky, irregular plates as it thickens. Bark color ranges from light gray to dark brown, orange, or red-burgundy over the course of the tree's life.

Needles: Needles grow in clusters of 3 and reach between 8 and 18 inches (20–45.7 cm) in length. They tend to be tufted at the ends of branches, have a feathery surface, and are a vivid green.

Cones: Pollination occurs in early spring with male cones reaching 1.2–3.1 in (3–8 cm) long. Female seed cones mature 20 months after pollination and are yellow-brown in color when mature. They can reach 6–10 in (15–25 cm) in length and 2–2.8 in (5–7 cm) in width, opening to 4.7 in (12 cm). In the middle of each scale is a small, sharp downward-pointing spine.

The longleaf pine, also known as the longleaf yellow pine or southern yellow pine, produces many long-needled and dense fascicles of needles, which is the source of its name. At the end of each branch is a "foliar unit," or a ball of needles; clustered in the center of these units are silvery-white buds that can grow from 3 to 15 in (7.6–38 cm) long and aid in identification of the tree. The tree shape is generally rounded and erect although its branches tend to be twisted or gnarled. Its wood is often used as lumber and its needles as pine straw, while the sap of the tree was used to make tar that sealed the wood of boats. It is the state tree of Alabama. *Pinus palustris* has some of the largest cones among the pine species.

INTERESTING FACTS

• Longleaf pine was historically often used for naval purposes, specifically for turpentine, tar, resin, and pitch.

• Due to its high flammability rating, the longleaf pine is not suitable for planting around a home.

• The Imperial Moth (*Eacles imperialis*) larvae depend on the longleaf pine for their brood season.

• The oldest known tree was found at the Weymouth Woods Sandhills Nature Preserve, North Carolina, it was estimated to be at least 460 years old.

• The seeds are a food source for many types of wildlife, including fox and gray squirrels, turkeys, and mourning doves.

HABITAT AND DISTRIBUTION

Habitat
Pinus palustris does best in full sun, in clay or well-drained sandy soils. Susceptible to storm and ice damage, the tree is also intolerant of drought, high winds, or lightning. The tree's epithet *palustris* is Latin, translating to "of the marsh," which is indicative of the species' common habitat. The pine grows in warm, wet temperate climates characterized by mild winters and hot summers.

Distribution
The longleaf pine is native to the southeast including most of the Atlantic and Gulf Coastal Plains and can be found between southeastern Virginia, west to eastern Texas, and south to the northern two-thirds of Florida. The species also grows in the Mountain Provinces, Ridge and Valley, and Piedmont of northwest Georgia and Alabama. *Pinus palustris* is typically found in coastal and woodland landscapes, as well as naturalized areas.

PONDEROSA PINE
Pinus ponderosa

Avg height: 60–200 ft
Avg trunk diameter: 30–50 in (76–127 cm)
Lifespan: 400–500 years

Bark: Young trees, referred to as "blackjacks" by early loggers, have blackish-brown bark. Mature trees have orange-red to yellow bark in very broad plates with black crevices.

Needles: The pine's five subspecies can be identified by their characteristically bright green needles, which have a wide range in size. The shortest belong to the central High Plains subspecies, averaging 2.2–2.8 in (5.6–7.1 cm) while the longest belong to the Pacific subspecies reaching up to 10 in (25.5 cm).

Cones: Between the subspecies, mature cones range in color from apple green, yellow green, red-brown, to dark purple. Cones are conical or egg-shaped and range 2–6 in (5–15 cm) in length. In contrast to the Jeffrey pine, which has similar features, the cones of *Pinus ponderosa* are armed with straight prickles.

Pinus ponderosa, also known as the ponderosa pine, filipinus pine, western yellow pine, blackjack pine, or bull pine, is a very large tree that is the most widely distributed pine species in North America. The trunk is straight with an open, wide, irregularly cylindrical crown. First documented in 1826 in eastern Washington, it was adopted as the state tree of Montana in 1949. The tree has five subspecies: Pacific (*P. p. critchfieldiana*), Columbia (*P. p. ponderosa*), Rocky Mountains (*P. p. scopulorum*), Southwestern (*P. p. brachyptera*), and Central High Plains (*P. p. readiana*), which can be distinguished by measurements of needles and seed cones, as well as the color of mature cones. These subspecies have differing botanical characters and adaptations to their varying climates.

INTERESTING FACTS

• In 1953, 145 ponderosa pines were used in a nuclear test during Operation Upshot-Knothole, where the trees were transported and planted at Area 5 of the Nevada Test Site to observe what effects a blast wave would have on a forest.

• In 1908, a poll was taken by Montana schoolchildren to determine the state tree, and the ponderosa pine was chosen over cottonwood, American larch, and the Douglas fir.

• After being introduced to New Zealand, *Pinus ponderosa* spread as an invasive species, driving out native species in certain areas.

HABITAT AND DISTRIBUTION

Habitat
Ponderosa pine grows best in deep, moist, well-drained soil and full sun, but can adapt to a wide range of soil and growing conditions including high elevation, wind, low humidity, and dry or alkaline soils. Due to the number of subspecies, the tolerance of different climates, topographies, and soils has a wide range.

Distribution
Because there are five subspecies of ponderosa pine, the range is extensive and is one of the most widely distributed pines in North America. The tree can be found between southern Canada into Mexico and from the Pacific Coast to the Plains States of Nebraska and Oklahoma.

TABLE MOUNTAIN PINE
Pinus pungens

Avg height: 20–65 ft (6–19.8 m)
Avg trunk diameter: 12–18 in
(30.5–45.7 cm)
Lifespan: 150 years

Bark: The tree's bark is broken by fissures into irregular plates. The texture ranges from nearly smooth to flaky, with the thickness of the bark increasing as the diameter of the trunk increases.

Needles: Needles are deep yellow-green in color and grow in clusters of 2 per fascicle, which are retained for 2–3 years. The needles range from 1.3–4 in (3.3–10 cm) in length.

Cones: The scales of the cones are armed with broad, upwardly curving spines. Male cones grow to around 0.6 in (1.5 cm) long, while female cones range from 1.7–4 in (4.2–10 cm) in length. The size of cones' length decreases as elevation increases.

Pinus pungens, also known as hickory pine, mountain pine, or prickly pine, is a small pine with a rounded, irregular shape. Younger trees can vary in form from a slender tree with small limbs to a large bush depending on whether or not it is open-grown or in a dense stand, while older trees become more flat-topped. The trunks of the pine have irregularly shaped cross-sections and are often crooked and have thick, long, low-lying limbs on much of the trunk. Compared to other pine species in the area, its pollen is released early, which minimizes hybridization of the species. The table mountain pine also differs from other pines in that it commonly grows as small groves or single scattered trees, rather than in large forests. The wood of this tree is often used for pulpwood and firewood.

INTERESTING FACTS

• The table mountain pine is the Lonesome Pine of John Fox's novel "The Trail of the Lonesome Pine," which was also referenced in the Laurel and Hardy film "Way out West."

• Although most table mountain pines rarely grow above 66 ft (20 m) tall, there is a specimen in Stokes County, North Carolina, that is recorded to have reached 95 ft (29 m) in height with a trunk diameter of 34 in (94 cm), nearly double the average.

HABITAT AND DISTRIBUTION

Habitat
The table mountain pine, unlike other pines that are in dense forests, grow either scattered or in small groves. They are often found in pure stands or co-dominant with pitch pine or Virginia pine, which grow well together. Frequently found on ridges of gorges that dissect the Blue Ridge Mountains, the pine is tolerant of a range of elevations.

Distribution
Pinus pungens is native to the Appalachian Mountains. Found primarily in the Blue Ridge and Valley-and-Ridge provinces of the Appalachian Highlands, its range extends southwest from central Pennsylvania to eastern West Virginia, and southward into Tennessee, North Carolina, and northeast Georgia.

PINE CONES

In the pine family, the male (pollinating) and female (seed-bearing) parts are carried on cones; it is the woody female cone that is used to identify different pine species, as the male part is small and rarely seen. The *Pinus* (hard pine) and *Strobus* (soft pine) subgenera in the *Pinus* genus are further broken down. The longest and largest cones can be found in the white pine group (*Quinquefolia*) of the *Strobus* subgenus, while the small, globose Pinyon cone (*Parrya*) is the source of pine nuts. Many cones open to release their seeds as soon as they mature; this is true of all *Strobus* and many in the *Pinus* subgenus. Some cones, however, are serotinous, covered in a resin that must be melted by a forest fire before they can release their seeds (for example, Lodgepole, Jeffrey, and Ponderosa Pines).

Once cones mature and open to release their seeds, they then open or close depending on the amount of moisture in the air; if it is wet or humid, the scales close to protect the seeds; if it's dry, they open to release the seeds. Even after all the seeds are gone, the cone continues to open or shut depending on moisture in the air or, if they have fallen, on the ground.

Red Pine *Pinus resinosa*
Pinus/Pinus
serotinous or open at maturity

Lodgepole Pine *Pinus contorta*
Pinus/Trifoliae
serotinous

Shortleaf Pine *Pinus echinata*
Pinus/Trifoliae
open at maturity

Ponderosa Pine *Pinus ponderosa*
Pinus/Trifoliae
serotinous

Table Mountain Pine *Pinus pungens*
Pinus/Trifoliae
open at maturity

Pitch Pine *Pinus rigida*
Pinus/Trifoliae
open at maturity

Pinyon *Pinus edulis*
Strobus/Parrya
globose cones with a few thick scales;
opens at maturity and holds the seeds
on the scales

Limber Pine *Pinus flexilis*
Strobus/Quinquefolia
bright green when immature;
thick scales
open at maturity

Sugar Pine *Pinus lambertiana*
Strobus/Quinquefolia
longest cones of any conifer
open at maturity

Slash Pine *Pinus elliottii*
Pinus/Trifoliae
open at maturity

Spruce Pine *Pinus glabra*
Pinus/Trifoliae
open at maturity

Jeffrey Pine *Pinus jeffreyi*
Pinus/Trifoliae
serotinous

Longleaf Pine *Pinus palustris*
Pinus/Trifoliae
open at maturity

Pond Pine *Pinus serotina*
Pinus/Trifoliae
pollination (male) cones

Loblolly Pine *Pinus taeda*
Pinus/Trifoliae
open at maturity

Virginia Pine *Pinus virginiana*
Pinus/Trifoliae
young female cone receptive for pollination

Western White Pine *Pinus monticola*
Strobus/Quinquefolia
long, slender cones with thin and flexible scales
open at maturity

Eastern White Pine *Pinus strobus*
Strobus/Quinquefolia
Scales have rounded apex and slightly reflexed
tip, and are often resinous open at maturity

Tamarack *Larix laricina*
open at maturity

Western Larch *Larix occidentalis*
open at maturity

RED PINE

Pinus resinosa

Named by William Aiton in 1789, *Pinus resinosa*, also known as red pine, Norway pine, or pin rouge, is a conical, straight-trunked evergreen coniferous species of tree native to Canada that can be found in northeastern states. The trunk of the red pine supports a dense, symmetrical, and oval crown that is supported by upward-curving branches. It is the state tree of Minnesota and was once an important timber pine in the Great Lakes region, referred to as the "Norway pine" by the men who logged it. Red pine has been used commercially in forestry for structural timber and pulpwood and is also used for landscaping.

Avg height: 60–80 ft (18.3–24.3 m)
Avg trunk diameter: 24–36 in (61–91 cm)
Lifespan: 400–500 years

Bark: The bark is furrowed and cross-checked into irregularly rectangular, scaly plates that are light red-brown in color, giving the tree its common name of red pine.

Needles: Needles are straight and slightly twisted, growing in groups of two needles per fascicle. They grow to 4.8–7.2 in (12–18 cm) in length, are a deep yellow-green in color, and are rather brittle.

Cones: Pollen cones are a dark purple color and grow to around 0.6 in (15 mm) in length with an ellipsoid shape. Seed cones mature 2 years after pollination and change from ovoid to nearly globose once open. They can grow 1.5–2.5 in (3.5–6 cm) in length and are a light red-brown color.

INTERESTING FACTS

• The origin of the name "Norway" pine in Minnesota may stem from early Scandinavian immigrants who saw similarities between the American red pines and their native Scots pines.

• Older trees may have long lengths of branchless trunk below the canopy as the species is self pruning, with very few dead branches remaining on the trees.

• Red pine is heavily reliant on fire for regeneration and has natural fire defenses. Fire reduces damage to cones and seeds from insects, kills surrounding competition, and prepares seedbeds by burning litter on the ground.

HABITAT AND DISTRIBUTION

Habitat
The species grows mainly in boreal forests and naturally occurs on sandy soils at elevations of 650–4,200 ft (200–1,300 m) above sea level. Best growth occurs in cool summer climates, as the trees often struggle in areas where summers are hot.

Distribution
While *Pinus resinosa* is native to Canada, it can be found in the northeastern U.S. along the Canadian border, including Maine, New Hampshire, Vermont, and New York, down to Massachusetts, Connecticut, New Jersey, Pennsylvania, West Virginia, and west to Michigan, Illinois, Wisconsin, and Minnesota.

PITCH PINE
Pinus rigida

Avg height: 20–100 ft (6–31 m)
Avg trunk diameter: 24–48 in (61–122 cm)
Lifespan: 100–200 years

Bark: The bark is deeply and irregularly furrowed with long, flat, rectangular ridges and resin pockets. The bark is red-brown in color, changing to almost black as the tree ages.

Needles: The stiff, slightly twisted needles grow in fascicles of three and reach 2.25–5 in (6–13 cm) in length. Compared to other pines, the needles are rather stout, over .04 in (1 mm) wide. Needles turn from yellow-green to dark-green in color as the tree matures.

Pollen cones: Cylindrical pollen cones are yellow in color and grow to 0.8 in (20 mm) in length.

Seed cones: Seed cones are symmetrically conic before opening and broadly ovoid when open. They are a creamy brown to light red-brown in color, and grow to around 1.2–3.5 in (3–9 cm) in length.

The pitch pine, named *Pinus rigida* by British botanist Philip Miller, is a small-to-medium-sized pine that is found in environments that many other species would find unsuitable for growth. Irregular in shape, the branches of the pitch pine are often twisted and the tree does a poor job at self-pruning. Twisting, gnarled, and drooping branches create this irregularity. The needles of the pine are exceptionally stiff, as described in the species name *rigida*. Due to the tree often sporting multiple or crooked trunks, it is considered to be a low-grade timber species. The common name of pitch pine refers to the tree's high resin content and pine knots served as torches when fastened to a pole, while colonists produced tar and turpentine from the wood. It is a hardy species of tree and is known as a pioneer species as it is often the first tree to vegetate a site after it has been cleared away.

INTERESTING FACTS

• The wood's high resin content protects it from decay, causing the tree to be a major source of timber and pitch for railroad ties, mine timbers, and ship building.

• In Ismaning and Muehlaker Germany, pitch pine wood was used for building radio towers.

• The Native American nations of Iroquois, Shinnecock, and Cherokee used pitch pine for medicinal purposes, as a laxative as well as a poultice to treat boils, burns, rheumatism, and cuts.

HABITAT AND DISTRIBUTION

Habitat
Pitch pine grows on sterile soils that range from dry to boggy, on upland or lowland sites. Elevation ranges from sea level to 4,800 ft (1,400 m). Pitch pine is a hardy tree, resistant to fire and injury, and is suited to grow in dry rocky soils that is not tolerated by other trees and the inherent exposure increases the tree's open and irregular shape.

Distribution
In addition to being native to Canada, the pitch pine can be found in Georgia, South Carolina, North Carolina, Tennessee, Kentucky, West Virginia, Virginia, Ohio, Maryland, Pennsylvania, Delaware, New Jersey, New York, Connecticut, Rhode Island, Massachusetts, Vermont, New Hampshire, and Maine.

POND PINE

Pinus serotina

Avg height: 70–82 ft (21–25 m)
Avg trunk diameter: 24–28 in (61–71 cm)
Lifespan: 100–200 years

Pinus serotina, named by André Michaux in 1803, and more commonly known as the pond pine, marsh pine, or pocosin pine, can be found along the southeastern portion of the Atlantic coastal plain. The species name, *serotina*, means "late" and is derived from the tree's cones, which remain persistently unopened for years before releasing seeds; often, this opening is in response to forest fire. The tree has an irregular crown and a crooked growth pattern with a trunk that is often crooked with adventitious sprouts. As the tree ages, the crowns often become thin and ragged, flat, or broadly rounded.

INTERESTING FACTS

• One of the largest specimens of pond pines can be found in North Carolina, and is measured at 94 ft (29 m) in height with a trunk diameter of 37 in (94 cm) and a crown spread of 46 ft (14 m).

• The pond pine is particularly resistant to wildfires and can produce sprouts from the roots after a fire; even after being entirely consumed by a fire, the species is able to re-sprout.

Bark: Bark is irregularly furrowed and cross-checked into flat, scaly plates that are red-brown in color.

Needles: Needles grow spreading to ascending in bunches of 3 per fascicle and may grow directly from the trunk. They persist on the tree for 2–3 years and measure up to 6–8 in (15–20 cm) in length. They are yellow-green in color and grow with a slight twist, growing in tufts at the ends of twigs.

Cones: Pollen cones are yellow-brown in color and reach up to 1.8 in (30 mm) in length, while seed cones are pale red-brown to creamy brown in color and reach 2–3.2 in (5–8 cm) in length. Cones remain unopened for years after pollination and often open only as a result of a fire.

HABITAT AND DISTRIBUTION

Habitat
The pond pine grows in a wide range of soil types, including damp and wet soil with poor drainage. Its native habitat includes ponds, shallow bays, flatwoods, flatwoods bogs, savannas, barrens, and swamps. The tree can be found at elevations between sea level to 650 ft (200 m) and can tolerate cold temperatures between 10° and 20°F (-12.1° and -6.7°C).

Distribution
Found along the southeastern portion of the Atlantic coastal plain, the species is native to Alabama, Florida, Georgia, South Carolina, North Carolina, Virginia, Maryland, Delaware, and New Jersey.

EASTERN WHITE PINE
Pinus strobus

Avg height: 150–210 ft (45–64 m)
Avg trunk diameter: 36–60 in (91–152 cm)
Lifespan: 200–400 years

Bark: On young trees, the bark is smooth, thin, and gray-green in color with lighter patches. As the tree matures, the bark darkens to brown or gray-brown and thickens, forming long, rounded, prominent ridges of scales and dark furrows.

Needles: The needles of *Pinus strobus* grow in fascicles of 5 and are bluish-green in color. Finely serrated, the needles are flexible and grow to around 2–5 in (5–13 cm) in length and persist on the tree for 2–3 years.

Cones: The seed cones of the eastern white pine are slender, reaching around 3.25–6.24 in (8–16 cm) in length, and are 1.5–2 in (4–5 cm) when open. The scales of the cones have a rounded apex and a tip that is bent back slightly.

Pinus strobus, or the eastern white pine, also known as soft pine, Weymouth pine, white pine, northern white pine, and eastern white pine is the state tree of both Michigan and Maine. Its form is pyramidal in its early years, maturing to a broad oval with an irregular crown. Branches are spaced evenly on the trunk, about every 18 inches, with 5–6 branches growing like spokes on a wheel. *Pinus strobus* grows well in cool summer locations, but is susceptible to a number of disease and insect problems. The white pine blister rust is the main enemy, as it is usually fatal. Insect problems include aphids, scale, pine sawfly, Zimmerman moth larvae, white pine shoot borer, bark beetles, and white pine weevil. As it is a dominant tree in mixed forests, it provides food and shelter for numerous forest birds including the red crossbill, as well as many small mammals.

INTERESTING FACTS

• The Haudenosaunee (Iroquois) nation called it the "Tree of Peace" and its bundles of five needles became the symbol given to the creation of the Five Nations joined as one.

• It is occasionally referred to as the "Weymouth pine" after Captain George Weymouth of the British Royal Navy returned to England from Maine with seeds of the pine in 1605.

• *Pinus strobus* forests used to cover much of northeastern and north-central North America; as a result of extensive logging in the 18th-20th centuries, only one percent of the old-growth forests remain. Today, these forests are protected in Great Smoky Mountains National Park.

HABITAT AND DISTRIBUTION

Habitat
The eastern white pine grows well in well-drained, medium moisture, acidic soil in full sun. It prefers cool, humid climates and fertile soils, and is intolerant of alkaline conditions and compacted, clayey soils. Additionally, it is intolerant of many air pollutants such as ozone and sulfur dioxide. In mixed forests, this dominant pine often towers over others.

Distribution
The eastern white pine grows in the near-arctic temperate broadleaf and mixed forests biome of eastern North America. It occurs west from Newfoundland, Canada, through the Great Lakes region to southeastern Minnesota and Manitoba, and south along the Appalachian Mountains and upper Piedmont to north Georgia. Rarely, it can occur in higher elevations in northeastern Alabama and is considered rare in Indiana.

LOBLOLLY PINE
Pinus taeda

Avg height: 100–115 ft (30–35 m)
Avg trunk diameter: 1.3–5 ft (40–1.52 cm)
Lifespan: 150–275 years

Bark: The bark of a young tree is red-brown to gray-brown and scaly. As the tree matures, the bark thickens and forms irregular, flaky plates that are somewhat rounded, leaving the tree ridged and furrowed. When removed, the bark reveals a dark chocolate color of the wood underneath.

Needles: Needles grow in bunches of three and measure between 5–10 in (12.5–25 cm) in length, persisting for two years on the tree. The needles are finely-toothed, slender and stiff, and yellow-green to dark green in color.

Cones: Seed cones grow between 2.75–5 in (7–13 cm) in length and are 0.75–1.25 in (2–3 cm) when closed, widening to 1.5–2.25 in (4–6 cm) once open. The scales of the cones have a sharp spine 3–6 mm long and the cones are green in color when first formed, aging to a pale buff-brown.

The loblolly pine is the second-most common species of tree in the U.S. following the red maple. Native to the southeast, the species is regarded as the most commercially important tree to the region. The wood industry classifies the species as a southern yellow pine and the tree was given its common name of loblolly due to its tendency to grow in swampy areas and lowlands. The resinous wood is prized for lumber as well as being used for wood pulp. Noted for its particularly straight trunk it loses its lower branches and gradually develops a dense oval-rounded crown as it matures. The seeds of the tree are an important food source for small mammals and more than 20 songbirds, making up for over half of the diet of the red crossbill. Loblolly stands provide habitat and cover for gray and fox squirrels, wild turkey, northern bobwhite, and white-tailed deer.

INTERESTING FACTS

• The tallest and largest known loblolly pines are found in Congaree National Park in South Carolina, measuring 169 ft (51.4 m) tall and 1,500 cu ft (42 m³) in volume respectively.

• Seeds of the loblolly pine were carried aboard the Apollo 14 flight and upon the flight's return planted in several locations including the White House grounds. These trees are referred to as moon trees.

• Each year, three-quarters of a million acres (300,000 ha) are harvested for pulpwood and lumber; most harvested pines are less than 50 years old.

• Old-growth loblolly pines provide nesting habitat for the endangered red-cockaded woodpecker.

HABITAT AND DISTRIBUTION

Habitat
The loblolly pine has no tolerance for shade and grows best in full sun and medium to wet soils. It prefers moist, acidic soils with poor drainage and climates with hot and humid summers and mild winters. The species grows in elevations from sea level to 2,400 ft (31.5 m) in a variety of conditions. The tree typically grows in pure stands and has the most rapid growth rate of any pine.

Distribution
Native to the southeast, the loblolly pine can be found from eastern Texas east to Florida and north to southern New Jersey. The tree can also be found in southern Tennessee, central Arkansas, and southeastern Oklahoma, as well as the Valley-and-Ridge Province of the Appalachian Highlands, the southern extent of the Cumberland Plateau, the Atlantic Coastal Plain, and the Piedmont Plateau.

Avg height: 18–59 ft (5–18 m)
Avg trunk diameter: 8–20 in (20–50 cm)
Lifespan: 65–100 years

Bark: On young trees, the bark is scaly and orange-brown in color. As the tree ages, the tree develops small, thin, scaly plates, and cinnamon-colored patches often appear on upper parts of the trunk. The bark is thin compared to other pines, making it poorly adapted to fire.

Needles: The relatively short and twisted needles, which grow in bunches of two, are a key characteristic. They grow to 0.78–3.15 in (2–8 cm) in length and are yellow-green in color. Needles persist 3–4 years on the tree.

Cones: Unlike some other pines, *Pinus virginiana* produces cones in all parts of the canopy. Pollen cones are circular and are 0.4–0.8 in (1–2 cm) in size and are typically the same color as the bark. Mature seed cones are 1.6–2.7 in (4–7 cm) in length, much larger than the pollen cones, and are red-brown in color. Cone scales are rigid with a strong purple-red or purple-brown border.

VIRGINIA PINE
Pinus virginiana

Pinus virginiana, commonly known as the Virginia pine, Jersey pine, and scrub pine, is a medium-sized tree with flexible branches that is useful for reforesting and provides important nourishment for a number of wildlife. It is also used for lumber and wood pulp. Older trees that suffer from stem rot provide particularly good nesting sites for woodpeckers. In the southern and middle Appalachian region, the tree is widely planted to revegetate surface coal mine spoils. When used for revegetation, the tree has high value for food and wildlife cover and is particularly important for foraging white-tailed deer. When young, the tree grows as a broad, open pyramid, becoming horizontal and flat-topped as the tree ages.

INTERESTING FACTS

• The Native American Cherokee nation used *Pinus virginiana* for medical purposes, treating constipation, hemorrhoids, diarrhea, tuberculosis, colds, fevers, and stiffness of the body. It was also used in certain cultural rituals, including burials and wind prayers.

• Historically, the lumber of the Virginia pine was used as mine timbers, for railroad ties, and for fuel and tar. Today, the wood is also used for lumber and wood pulp, which is used to make paper.

• The tallest known Virginia pine is located in the watershed of Morsingills Creek, Georgia, measured at 122 ft (37.28 m), standing only a few feet from the tallest known *Pinus rigida*.

HABITAT AND DISTRIBUTION

Habitat
Pinus virginiana commonly inhabits dry forested areas and tends to grow in pure stands rather than mixed groups. The tree prefers well-drained clay or loam but is capable of growing on very poor, sandy soil, although this affects the growth of the tree and will often remain stunted and small. While the tree is poorly adapted to fire due to its shallow roots and thin bark, larger trees are able to survive.

Distribution
The tree can be found from Long Island in southern New York occurring in New Jersey and Pennsylvania, south through the Appalachian Mountains to Alabama and western Tennessee, and west to Ohio, Kentucky, and Indiana.

CUPRESSACEAE

Although they are conifers—softwoods that bear their seeds in cones—none in the Cypress family has cones that resemble those that are typically associated with the term "pine cone," but instead has a modified version, such as the juniper "berry," actually a cone with fleshy scales that grow together. Nearly all of the Cupressaceae have compressed, scalelike leaves, with the exception of the tallest tree in the world—the Coast Redwood—which has needles.

CHAMAECYPARIS (FALSE CYPRESS)

JUNIPERUS (JUNIPER)

FORM False-cypresses, which include the Port Orford-cedar, are tall, pyramidal trees with bark that is smooth or peeling off in strips, and leatherly, scalelike foliage that grows in flat sprays.

REPRODUCTION The globose cones have 8 to 14 scales arranged in opposite pairs. Each scale has 2 to 4 seeds, so the larger cones may have up to 56 seeds, which are released when the cone opens.

FORM Junipers can thrive in a variety of habitats and on different substrates, and their form and shape varies from shrub to trees that are shaped by environmental stresses such as high winds.

REPRODUCTION Juniper berries are actually cones in which the scales are fleshy and have grown together into a single, unified covering for up to four seeds. They are hard when immature but soften at maturation.

THUJA (WHITECEDAR/REDCEDAR)

SEQUOIA (REDWOOD)

FORM Also known as Thujas or Arborvitae, these can grow up to 200 feet tall and have reddish-brown, stringy bark. They are often dense and conical to narrow-pyramidal, they may mature to broad pyramidal.

REPRODUCTION The upright woody cones, with 2–3 pairs of opposite decussate scales, ending in a hooked point, which turn brown and open like flowers when they mature, releasing 8 red-brown seeds.

FORM Coast redwoods are the tallest trees in the world, reaching more than 380 feet tall, and comparatively slender for their height with a trunk only 30 feet wide; the crown is conical, with horizontal or drooping branches.

REPRODUCTION The cones are ovoid to globose, with 15–25 spirally arranged scales, each with 3–7 tiny winged seeds—and are perhaps most noted for their diminutive size despite the great size of the Redwood.

Avg height: 64–128 ft (20–40 m)
Avg trunk diamater: 8–24 in (20–60 cm)
Lifespan: 300–500 years

Bark: The bark ranges from light green to light gray as the tree ages. On mature trees, the bark becomes irregularly furrowed and may exfoliate. Bark reaches 0.4–0.8 in (1–2 cm) thick.

Needles: The dark green scutiform leaves are 1.2–2 in (3–5 mm) long and emerge in flat clusters. The leaves are imbricated, wedge-shaped, flat, rough, and green.

Cones: Cones have 4 scales and resemble the cones of the Mexican cypress (*Cupressus lusitanica*). The cones are typically 0.4–0.5 in (1–1.4 cm) in diameter. Each scale has a pointed triangular bract about 1.5–2 mm long.

ALASKA CEDAR
Callitropsis nootkatensis

Callitropsis nootkatensis, also known as Alaska cedar, Alaska yellow cedar, yellow cedar, Nootka cedar, Alaska cypress, yellow cypress, and Nootka cypress, is a medium-sized, evergreen conifer. The name "nootkatensis" is derived from its discovery on the lands of the Nuu-chah-nulth people of Vancouver Island, British Columbia by Europeans. The Nuu-chah-nulth people of the First Nation of Canada were formerly referred to as the Nootka. It forms a strongly weeping, pyramidal tree. Trailing curtains of dark green foliage hang from upward-sweeping spreading branches.

INTERESTING FACTS

• The wood was used medicinally to cure common colds, minimize skin eruptions, and reduce circulatory problems.

• The wood is one of the most desired sources of heat on the west coast as it has extreme heartwood qualities and burns very hot for a long period of time.

• The species was exported to China during the last century because it is considered to be one of the finest timber trees in the world, with its wood often being used for flooring, interior finish, and shipbuilding.

HABITAT AND DISTRIBUTION

Habitat
It typically appears in humid places in the mountains, often near the treeline, but sometimes also at lower elevations. They prefer moist, well-drained, and somewhat acidic soils, a species typical of cool and humid climates, and do not thrive well in low-lying areas or on the coast.

Distribution
The Alaska cedar is native to the west coast of North America, from the Kenai Peninsula in Alaska south to the northern tip of California.

PORT-ORFORD CEDAR
Chamaecyparis lawsoniana

Chamaecyparis lawsoniana, often known as Port-Orford cedar or Lawson cypress, is a coniferous plant in the *Chamaecyparis* genus of the Cupressaceae family. The Port-Orford cedar is an evergreen tree that is large and uniform with a pyramidal-shaped crown with frondlike branches. The wood is light yet strong and resistant to decay. Its timber is also recognized for having a strong ginger scent. It is one of the most popular woods for making arrow shafts due to the straightness of its grain, and, for the same reason, it is used in the making of stringed instruments. For soundboards in guitars, the fine grain, robustness, and tonal qualities of Port-Orford cedar are highly valued.

Avg height: 100–200 ft (30.5–61 m)
Avg trunk diameter: 45–80 in (115–200 cm)
Lifespan: 600–1,000 years

Bark: The bark of a mature tree is ridged, fibrous, and deeply furrowed. Near the base of the trunk, the bark can reach 4–8 in (10–20 cm) thick.

Needles: Needles are scale-like and reach 3–5 mm) in length. They grow on flattened stems with faint white lines on the underside. The leaves have a strong parsley-like fragrance.

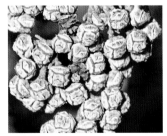

Cones: Seed cones are globose with a diameter of 0.25–0.5 in (0.7–1.4 cm), each with 6–10 scales. In early fall, the cones ripen and change from green to a rich brown, approximately 6–8 months after pollination. Male cones are 3–4 mm) long and dark crimson in color. Once pollen is released in early spring, they turn brown.

INTERESTING FACTS

• The wood is especially prized in East Asia, with considerable quantities exported to Japan where it is used to make coffins, shrines, and temples.

• Although the USDA and most people in its native area describe the species as Port-Orford cedar, some botanists prefer the term Lawson cypress.

• It was discovered at Port Orford, Oregon, in 1854, and put into cultivation by Charles Lawson FRSE's collectors.

HABITAT AND DISTRIBUTION

Habitat
Chamaecyparis lawsoniana grows best on moist, well-drained soils in a protected spot in full sun. Several hundred varieties with different crown shapes, growth rates, and leaf colors have been chosen for use in parks and gardens..

Distribution
Chamaecyparis lawsoniana is endemic to Oregon and northwestern California, where it grows in the valleys of the Klamath Mountains, frequently along streams, from sea level to 4,900 ft (1,500 m).

ATLANTIC WHITECEDAR
Chamaecyparis thyoides

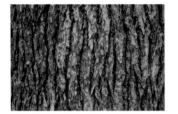

Avg height: 65–90 ft (20–28 m)
Avg trunk diamater: 30–70 in
(80–200 cm)
Lifespan: 200–1,000 years

Bark: The bark of the Atlantic whitec edar ranges from ash-gray to reddish-brown. The bark is smooth on young trees, but mature trees have deep ridges and bark as thick as 2 in (5 cm). Its wood is considered hardy because it is resistant to decay and warping in a variety of temperatures and moisture levels due to narrow grooves between the plates.

Needles: The leaves are feathery and are green to glaucous blue-green in color. They are produced in opposing decussate pairs. They are needlelike and reach 2–4 mm in length.

Cones: Pollen cones are dark brown and reach 2–4 mm in length. Seed cones are often irregular or assymmetrical and mature and open within the first year. They are 4–9 mm wide and are bluish-purple to reddish-brown. Each cone has 6–8 scales, with each scale holding 1–2 seeds.

Chamaecyparis thyoides, also known as Atlantic Whitecedar, Atlantic white cypress, southern Whitecedar, or false-cypress, is one of North America's two *Chamaecyparis* species. *C. thyoides* is found on the East Coast, while *C. lawsoniana* is found on the West Coast. As a result of its extensive north-south distribution, the Atlantic Whitecedar is connected with a wide range of other wetland species. Residual populations are primarily in distant regions where harvesting would be difficult, so its appeal as a source of timber has declined. The Atlantic whitecedar is protected in the Great Dismal Swamp National Wildlife Refuge, Alligator River National Wildlife Refuge, Cape Cod National Seashore, and Croatan National Forest. The tree is classified as rare in Georgia and New York, special concern in Maine, and extirpated in Pennsylvania.

INTERESTING FACTS

• While it is commonly referred to as a cedar, *Chamaecyparis thyoides* is actually a cypress.

• Whitecedar charcoal was used to make gunpowder in the Revolutionary War.

• The most common use of the wood of the whitecedar is lumber, for which stands require 70 years of growth from germination to harvest.

HABITAT AND DISTRIBUTION

Habitat *Chamaecyparis thyoides* lives nearly entirely in freshwater marshes. It prefers to live in environments where the soil is wet for most of the growing season. These soils feature a thick organic layer with sandy material at deeper levels and poor drainage. The wetlands are acidic and there is very little oxygen in the soil because water has displaced the air. The plant thrives in marshes with wooded areas, where it tends to dominate the canopy.

Distribution
Chamaecyparis thyoides is native to the Atlantic coast of North America, where it can be found from southern Maine to Georgia, as well as the Gulf of Mexico coast from Florida to Mississippi. It grows up to 1,509 ft (460 m) above sea level in the foothills of the Appalachian Mountains, where rare populations can be discovered.

Avg height: 130–195 ft (40–60 m)
Avg trunk diameter: 39–55 in (100–140 cm)
Lifespan: 500–1,000 years

Bark: The bark ranges from orange-brown to gray as the tree ages. It starts smooth and over time develops irregular fissures, peeling off in large strips on the lower trunk. Wood is the most frequent material for wooden pencils since it is soft and sharpens rapidly without splinters.

Needles: Flattened sprays with scalelike leaves are 2–15 mm long. The leaves are grouped in opposing decussate pairs, with succeeding pairs closely then distantly separated, making apparent whorls of four. The facial pairs are flat, with the lateral pairs folded over their bases. On both sides of the branches, the leaves are vivid green, with only a few stomata visible. When crushed, the leaf emits a scent similar to that of shoe polish.

Cones: The seeds of the cones are .8–1.4 in (2–3.5 cm) long. The outer pair of scales each bears inner pairs and are fused in a flat plate. Pollen cones are between 3–8 mm.

INCENSE-CEDAR
Libocedrus decurrens

Incense-cedar grows in a pyramidal to narrowly conical shape and is frequently found bordering roads and pathways informal plantings. The incense-cedar is arguably the most well known of the Pacific Northwest native fake cedars, with its widespread usage in parks and landscaping. The incense-cedar, unlike the other natural fake cedars, favors drier, even drought-prone environments. The rich green foliage forms a luxuriant background in dry locations that is difficult to accomplish with other trees. The incense-cedar is one of California's most fire- and drought-resistant plants. *Syntexis libocedrii*, a kind of wood wasp that lays its eggs in the smoldering wood shortly after a forest fire, prefers this tree as its favorite host. Incense-cedar mistletoe (*Phoradendron libocedri*), a parasitic plant that may be seen hanging from the tree's branches, is also a resident.

INTERESTING FACTS

• The incense-cedar has been employed in several fire history studies as well as a variety of other dendroecological investigations, as well as some climate studies.

• The tree is used by Native Americans in California for traditional medicine, basket manufacturing, hunting bows, construction materials, and friction fire.

• Plant nurseries produce *Libocedrus decurrens* as attractive trees for use in gardens and parks.

HABITAT AND DISTRIBUTION

Habitat
Although the incense-cedar favors drier conditions in its natural environment, it may also thrive in wetter conditions. In cool summer climes, the tree is frequently cultivated in gardens and parks. It can produce a very narrow columnar crown in these regions, an unexplained result of the milder climatic circumstances that are uncommon in trees within its warm summer native habitat in the California Floristic Province.

Distribution
The range is mostly in the U.S., ranging south from midwestern Oregon to far western Nevada, south through California, with a minor part in northern Baja California in northwest Mexico. It rises from sea level to an elevation of 160–9,510 ft (50–2,900 m).

Avg height: 32–64 ft (10–20 m)
Avg trunk diameter: 24–36 in
(60–90 cm)
Lifespan: 350–500 years

Bark: The bark is unique compared to other junipers, being dark gray-brown, and fractured into small square plates that superficially resemble alligator skin. It can also have stringy vertical fissuring like other junipers.

Needles: Mature leaves are scalelike, 1–2.5 mm long, reaching 5 mm on lead shoots, and are 1–1.5 mm wide. They are grouped in opposing decussate pairs or whorls of three. Juvenile leaves are needlelike and 5–10 mm long on early seedlings alone.

Cones: The berrylike cones are 7–1.5 mm in diameter. They are green when young, becoming copper-colored with a pale waxy bloom as they age, and contain 2–6 seeds. They mature in around 18 months and are eaten by birds and animals. Male cones measure 4–6 mm in length and shed pollen in the spring. It is mostly dioecious, with each tree producing just one set of cones; however, some trees are monoecious.

ALLIGATOR JUNIPER
Juniperus deppeana

Juniperus deppeana, also known as alligator juniper or checkerbark juniper, táscate, and tláscal, is a small to medium-sized tree. Alligator juniper forms a broadly pyramidal or round-topped crown. The distinctive bark is furrowed into checkered plates, making it easy to identify. Its fragrant, dark blue-green, scalelike foliage and copper-colored fruit are other familiar characteristics. At the base of chopped stumps, new sprouts frequently emerge. Birds and animals devour the huge "berries." Large trees frequently have a grotesquely dead crown, with some branches dying and turning pale gray rather than dropping; some branches die in a vertical strip and continue to grow on the other side.

INTERESTING FACTS

• *Juniperus* has 30 species in North America and 43 recognized taxa in total.

• The alligator juniper is one of the biggest junipers found in the Southwest.

• Birds and mammals consume the berries and the tree is valuable for cover, providing habitat, nesting places, shade, and shelter for a variety of birds and other animals.

HABITAT AND DISTRIBUTION

Habitat
The alligator juniper occurs in various types of woodlands such as pine-oak, juniper-oak, and riparian woodlands. It generally grows as individual trees among other junipers, oaks, ponderosa pine, or understory plants.

Distribution
The alligator juniper is found in the southwest U.S., central and northern Mexico from Oaxaca northward, and in Arizona, New Mexico, and western Texas. It grows at moderate elevations of 2,460–8,860 ft (750–2,700 m).

WESTERN JUNIPER

Juniperus occidentalis

There are two closely related junipers in the western U.S., the western juniper and the Sierra juniper, that are generally identified only by the shape and size of the tree and its location. Some botanists consider these separate species, *Juniperus occidentalis* (western juniper) and *Juniperus grandis* (Sierra juniper), while other botanists consider the Sierra juniper a variety of the western juniper (*Juniperus occidentalis* var. *australis*). The branches of the western juniper are thick, ascending or spreading, and are often contorted or curved. At the ends of the heavy main branches grow the foliage branches, which form dense rounded tufts. Young trees form a pyramidal crown, becoming rounded and irregular in older trees.

Avg height: 12–50 ft (4–15 m)
Avg trunk diameter: 12–40 in (30–100 cm)
Lifespan: 800–1,000 years

Bark: On young trees, the bark is pink-brown and smooth. As the tree ages, the bark flakes and turns from gray to red-brown or brown, flaking and exfoliating in thin strips.

Leaves: Leaves on an adult tree are scalelike, measuring 1–2 mm) long and 1–1.5 mm) wide. They are arranged in opposite decussate pairs or whorls of three. On young trees, leaves are needlelike and measure 5–10 mm long.

Aleksandr Stepanov/SS

Nina B/SS

Cones: Seed cones are berrylike and mature within 2 years, changing from purple-red to blue or purple and reaching 5–10 mm) in diameter. There are 1–3 seeds per cone, which are released when the cone dries.

INTERESTING FACTS

• The oldest and largest specimen of western juniper is the Bennett juniper, found in the Stanislaus National Forest of California, which stands at 83.2 ft (26 m) with a diameter of 12.4 ft (3.88 m) and is estimated to be between 3,000–6,000 years old.

• Early settlers used the wood of the western juniper for firewood and fence posts.

• Northern Paiute Native Americans used the western juniper for shelter, medicine, and food. Extracts were used to treat boils, venereal disease, sore throats, and colds.

HABITAT AND DISTRIBUTION

Habitat
The western juniper is often found on rocky, dry sites where there is little competition from larger species.

Distribution
Juniperus occidentalis is found in the Juniper Dunes Wilderness in Washington near its northern range limit. It is commonly found in extreme northwest Nevada, northeastern California, southwestern Idaho, eastern and central Oregon, and southeastern Washington. The western juniper grows in mountains at elevations of 2,600–9,800 ft (800–3,000 m) above sea level, rarely down to 330 ft (100 m).

EASTERN REDCEDAR

Juniperus virginiana

Avg height: 16–66 ft (5–20 m)
Avg trunk diameter: 12–39 in (30–100 cm)
Lifespan: 500–1,000 years

Bark: The bark is soft and silvery, covering the single trunk. It is thin and fibrous, growing 5–16 mm thick and peeling off in narrow strips.

Needles: The foliage is fragrant and scalelike. It can be either coarse or fine-cut and varies in color from light green to dark green, to gray-green, or blue-green, to brown-green in winter. The leaves are arranged in opposite decussate pairs or occasionally whorls of three.

Cones: Seed cones are berrylike and are a dark purple-blue color with a white wax covering that gives an overall sky-blue color. The seed cones are 3–6 mm long and contain 1–3 seeds and mature 6–8 months after pollination. Pollen cones are 2–3 mm long and 15 mm broad and shed pollen in early spring or late winter.

Juniperus virginiana, commonly known as red cedar, eastern red cedar, Virginian juniper, eastern juniper, red juniper, and other regional names, is an evergreen, aromatic native juniper species found from southeastern Canada to the Gulf of Mexico, as well as east of the Great Plains. There are two varieties: *Juniperus virginiana* var. *virginiana*, which is the eastern redcedar, and *Juniperus virginiana* var. *silicicola*, known as Bailey's southern cedar or the southern or sand redcedar. The trunk of the eastern redcedar is buttressed at the base and often angled with a compact, columnar, narrow crown that sometimes becomes broad and irregular as the tree ages. Used in traditional ceremonies by Native Americans, the smoke of burning eastern juniper is said to drive away evil spirits. Historically, Native American peoples used juniper wood poles to demarcate agreed-upon tribal hunting grounds.

INTERESTING FACTS

- Bailey's Southern Cedar (*Juniperus virginiana* var. *silicicola*) occurs only along the Atlantic Coast from North Carolina through the north half of Florida and the Gulf Coast west to Texas. Some consider it a different species from the eastern redcedar.

- *Silicicola* means flint-dweller from comes from the Latin roots silex and and cola.

- Unlike the eastern redcedar, it has orange-brown bark, smaller cones (3–4 mm long), and the scale leaves are blunt at the tip.

HABITAT AND DISTRIBUTION

Habitat
The eastern redcedar commonly occurs in mixed stands with a variety of trees. In the northeastern United States, it is often found on rocky ridgetops. On dry uplands or abandoned farmlands, pure stands of eastern redcedar occur throughout its range.

Distribution
Juniperus virginiana can be found between Ontario east to Nova Scotia, south through the northern Great Plains to eastern Texas, and east to the Atlantic Coast and northern Florida. *Juniperus virginiana* var. *silicicola* is restricted to river sandbanks and coastal dunes south along the Atlantic Coast from North Carolina to Florida, and west along the Gulf Coast from Florida to Texas.

NORTHERN WHITECEDAR
Thuja occidentalis

Avg height: 20–40 ft (6–12 m)
Avg trunk Diameter: 17–60 in (45–152 cm)
Lifespan: 50–150 years

Bark: *Thuja occidentalis* has a brownish-red bark that starts to turn gray as these trees mature. It is 6–9 mm thick and is fibrous, fissured and forms in long strips.

Needles: The foliage forms in flat sprays with scalelike leaves 1–4 mm long and 1–2 mm wide, pointed, and dull yellow-green on both top and bottom.

Cones: Pollen cones reddish, 1–2 mm long. Seed cones are ovoid, slender, yellow-green ripening to brown, 9–14 mm long and 4–5 mm wide with six to eight overlapping scales, and around 8 seeds. Seeds are red-brown in color and reach 4–7 mm in length.

Thuja occidentalis, also known as swamp cedar, American arborvitae, and eastern arborvitae, is an evergreen coniferous tree. In spite of its name, it is a member of the cypress family, *Cupressaceae,* and is not a true cedar. While not listed as endangered, whitecedar populations are threatened by high deer numbers, because the deer rapidly strip the soft evergreen foliage, particularly during winter months. It is a dense conical or narrow-pyramidal tree but may mature to a broad-pyramidal shape. French settlers had given it the common name of arborvitae, from the Latin for "tree of life," because they had learned from Native Americans that it could be an effective treatment for scurvy.

INTERESTING FACTS

• The largest known specimen of northern Whitecedar can be found on South Manitou Island in Leelanau County, Michigan. The tree stands at 112 ft (34 m) tall with a 69 in (175 cm) diameter.

• The oldest known living specimen was estimated at 1,141 years old, while the oldest known dead specimen was found with 1,653 growth rings.

• Northern Whitecedar is an important tree in traditional Ojibwe culture and is one of the four plants of the Ojibwe medicine wheel. It is the subject of sacred legends, being considered a gift to humanity for its myriad uses, including medicine, construction, and craft.

HABITAT AND DISTRIBUTION

Habitat
Northern Whitecedar grows commonly in wet forests, being particularly abundant in coniferous swamps where other larger and faster-growing trees cannot compete successfully. It also occurs on other sites with reduced tree competition, such as cliffs. Northern whitecedars can be very long-lived trees in certain conditions, with notably old specimens growing on cliffs where they are inaccessible to deer and wildfire.

Distribution
The Northern Whitecedar is native to southeastern Canada and northeastern United States, with its range extending from southeastern Manitoba east through the Great Lakes region into Ontario, Québec, New York, Vermont, New Hampshire, Maine, Prince Edward Island, New Brunswick, and Nova Scotia. Isolated populations are also found in west-central Manitoba and to the south in Massachusetts, Connecticut, Ohio, Illinois, and in the Appalachian Mountains of West Virginia, Virginia, Maryland, Pennsylvania, North Carolina, Tennessee, and Kentucky.

WESTERN REDCEDAR
Thuja plicata

Avg height: 200–250 ft (60–76 m)
Avg trunk diameter: 10–23 ft (3–7 m)
Lifespan: 800–1,500 years

Bark: The Quinnault Lake Cedar was the largest redcedar in the world. When younger, the gray bark is striated into long, narrow strips that are often partially lifted up from the wood of the trunk and readily tear away.

Needles: The foliage forms flat sprays with scalelike leaves in opposite pairs, with successive pairs at 90 degrees. The individual leaves are 1–4 mm long and 1–2 mm broad on most foliage sprays, but up to 0.5 in (1.2 cm) long on strong-growing lead shoots.They are strongly aromatic, with a scent reminiscent of pineapple when crushed.

Cones: Cones are slender, 0.4–0.7 in (1–1.8 cm) long and 4–5 mm broad with 8–12 thin, overlapping scales. They are green to yellow-green, ripening brown in fall about six months after pollination, and open at maturity to shed the seeds. The seeds are 4–5 mm long and 1 mm broad, with a narrow papery wing down each side. The pollen cones are 3–4 mm long, red or purple in color, and shed yellow pollen in spring.

Western redcedar is an evergreen coniferous tree in the cypress family Cupressaceae. In spite of its name, it is not a true cedar. In the American horticultural trade, it is also known as the Giant Arborvitae. Western redcedar is the Provincial tree of British Columbia and has extensive applications for the indigenous First Nations of the Pacific Northwest and has been called the "cornerstone of northwest coast Indian culture." It is known by many names including Pacific red cedar, British Columbia cedar, canoe cedar, giant cedar, or just red cedar. *Plicata*, the species name, derives from a Greek word meaning "folded in plaits," which refers to the pattern of its small leaves. It is one of two arborvitaes native to North America. Coincidentally, Native Americans of the West Coast also address the cedar as "long life maker."

INTERESTING FACTS

• The foliage is an important food source for Roosevelt elk and black-tailed deer, especially in winter when other food sources are scarce.

• Western redcedar provides excellent cover for skunks, raccoons, bears, and other animals, which nest inside the trunk cavities of the tree.

• Western redcedar is one of the most shade-tolerant species in the Pacific Northwest and the Rocky Mountains.

• The Quinnault Lake Cedar, north of Aberdeen, Washington, had a wood volume of 17,650 cu ft (500 cu m) before it was destroyed by a number of storms in 2014 and 2016.

HABITAT AND DISTRIBUTION

Habitat
Western redcedar is also a riparian tree, growing in many forested swamps and streambanks in its range. The tree is shade-tolerant and able to reproduce under dense shade.

Distribution
Thuja plicata is one of the most widespread trees in the Pacific Northwest along the Pacific Coast from Alaska south to California, and British Columbia southeast into Idaho and western Montana, and is found from sea level to an elevation of 7,513 ft (2,290 m) at Crater Lake in Oregon. It is associated with Douglas fir and western hemlock in most areas where it grows.

Avg height: 15–50 ft (5–15 m)
Avg Trunk Diameter: 20–24 in (50–60 cm)
Lifespan: 300–500 years

PACIFIC YEW
Taxus brevifolia

Taxus brevifolia, also known as the Pacific or western yew and mountain mahogany, is an evergreen conifer native to the Pacific Northwest. The tree is relatively small and has an indistinct growth form. Trunks are usually asymmetrical and fluted and have a very slow growth rate; the crown is open-conical with branches ascendent to drooping. The seeds of the tree are consumed by birds and dispersed in their droppings. While they are a food source for birds, the seeds are poisonous to humans and the foliage is poisonous to cattle and horses. Although the wood of the Pacific yew was often used for handicrafts and furniture, it was often considered an impediment to the harvest of larger timber trees because they often grew in the undergrowth of old-growth forests. Many stands were cut down indiscriminately in order to access the larger trees.

INTERESTING FACTS

• Parts of the tree including the bark contain a chemical compound called paclitaxel, now brand name Taxol, which was later approved for use in chemotherapy against ovarian cancer, certain kinds of breast cancers, lung cancer, and AIDS-related cancer.

• Due to the slow growth rate of the tree, it has a tendency to rot from the inside out, leaving the tree hollow and making age determination very difficult to impossible.

• Native Americans used the very hard wood to make items that needed to be structurally sound, including bows, paddles for canoes, and fishhooks.

Bark: The bark is brown and scaly, as well as thin, about 6 mm. The inner bark is a reddish-purple color. Below the bark is a thin layer of off-white sap wood that covers the darker heartwood. On mature trees, the bark is a purple-brown color in shredded or peeling scales that vary widely in size.

HABITAT AND DISTRIBUTION

Habitat
Taxus brevifola grows in a variety of environment types and is shade tolerant, although it can grow in full sun. In moist environments the tree is likely to grow on slopes and ridgetops, while in drier environments it will be limited to stream sides. As the tree is shade tolerant, it often forms as undergrowth, growing along streams and providing shade. The tree can be found in elevations between sea level and 77,218 ft (2,200 m).

Foliage: The needles are single and arranged spirally, although they appear to grow in ranks of 2, twisted to align in two flat rows on either side of the stem, except from the erect leading shoots. They are yellow-green to dark green in color above and a paler gray-green below. The needles are apex pointed but not sharp and grow to around 0.4–1 in (1–2.5 cm) in length and 2–3 mm broad.

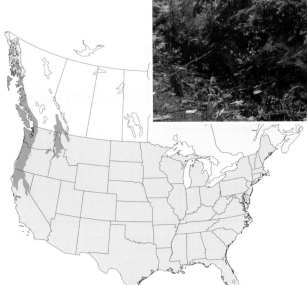

Fruit/Seed: Each seed cone contains a single seed about 0.25 in (0.6 cm) long. The seed is partly surrounded by a modified scale that develops into a soft berrylike structure called an aril; bright red in color, the oblong-oval aril is 0.25–0.5 in (0.6–1.25 cm) long and is open at the end where the seed sits. The arils mature 6–9 months after pollination.

Distribution
Native to the Pacific Northwest, the Pacific yew ranges from central California north to southernmost Alaska, predominantly in the Pacific Coast Ranges through Washington and Oregon. There are isolated disjunct populations of the tree that can be found in central to north Idaho and Montana.

CEDAR AND JUNIPER LEAVES AND CONES

The cedars and junipers—both in the cypress family—share tiny, scalelike leaves that are pressed close to the flat twigs . Unlike the large seed cones of the pine family, the seed cones of cypresses range from small woody spheres to cones with just a few scales that open from the base; the seed cones of junipers are actually within a berrylike covering. The male, pollen cones are often borne singly on the end of the twigs, while seed cones are borne in clusters farther up the branchlets.

Port-Orford Cedar
Chamaecyparis lawsoniana
Flat sprays of scalelike leaves 3–5 mm long with white markings on the underside. Seed cones 10–14mm in diameter, yellow-green cones turn brown; pollen cones red until pollen is released in spring, then turn brown.

Alaska-Cedar *Callinopteris nootkatensis*
Flat sprays of dark green scalelike leaves 3–5 mm long.
Seed cones 10–14 mm in diameter, yellow-green cones turn brown; pollen cones borne singly at end of twigs.

Atlantic Whitecedar *Chamaecyparis thyoides*
Moderately flattened sprays, 2–4 mm long scalelike leaves. Green or purple, globose cones turn brown; yellow pollen cones turn more brown as the tree matures.

Incense-Cedar *Calocedrus decurrens*
Scalelike leaves 2–15 mm long in opposite pairs in apparent whorls of four on flattened sprays. Seed cones, 20–35 mm, turn from pale green to orange-brown; the scales are in pairs with only the outer pair bearing seeds, which are winged. Orange pollen cones are 6–8 mm long.

Alligator-Juniper *Juniperus deppeana*
Scalelike leaves are in opposite pairs or whorls of three. Seed cones are berrylike, green maturing to orange-brown with a whitish waxy bloom at 18 months. Male cones yellow, 4–6 mm long. Dioecious: each tree produces only female or male cones.

Western Juniper *Juniperus occidentalis*
Scalelike leaves are in opposite pairs or whorls of three. Berrylike cones are blue-brown with a whitish bloom, mature at 18 months; the male cones are 2–4 mm. Half of trees are monoecious, with both male and female cones, half dioecious.

Eastern Redcedar *Juniperus virginiana*
Juvenile leaves are 5–10 mm long, needlelike, and spreading; adult leaves are 2–4 mm long, in opposite pairs or whorls of three. Seed cones are 3–7 mm, berrylike, dark purple, with a wax bloom; pollen cones are 2–3 mm long. Dioecious: each tree produces only female or male cones.

Northern Whitecedar *Thuja occidentalis*
Scalelike leaves in opposite pairs coming out at right angle to the previous pair form a fanlike spray. Seed cones are 9–14 mm long, yellow-green ripening to brown, with 6–8 overlapping scales. Yellow-green pollen cone, 3–4 mm long.

  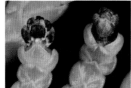

Western Redcedar *Thuja plicata*
Scalelike leaves in opposite pairs; each pair comes out at 90° angle to the previous pair. Seed cones 10–18 mm, yellow-green ripening to brown,, with 8–12 overlapping scales. Red or purple pollen cones, 3–4 mm long, have yellow pollen.

Avg height: 200–330 ft (60–100 m)
Avg trunk diameter: 120–180 in (305–457 cm)
Lifespan: 600–2,000 years

Bark: The bark can be very thick, around 12–14 in (30.5–35.5 cm), and is fibrous and rather soft. The bark is red-brown in color and forms broad, scaly ridges and deep furrows that cover inner bark, which is a cinnamon-brown color.

Foliage: Leaves are variable, growing 0.625–1 in (1.5–2.5 cm) long. On young trees and on the shaded lower branches of older trees, the leaves are flat. On shoots in full sun in the upper crown of older trees, the leaves are scalelike and reach 0.25–0.375 in (0.6–0.95 cm) in length. They are dark green above and have two blue-white stomatal bands below. Leaves grow in a spiral but larger shade trees are twisted and lie in a flat plane.

COAST REDWOOD
Sequoia sempervirens

Sequoia sempervirens, commonly known as the coast redwood, coastal redwood, and California redwood, is the sole living species of the genus *Sequoia* in the cypress family Cupressaceae. It includes the tallest living trees on earth, reaching up to 380 feet (115.8 m) in height and up to 29.2 feet (8.9 m) in trunk diameter. The tree has a conical crown with slightly drooping to horizontal branches. Due to factors including heavy rainfall in the tree's native area, the soil contains fewer nutrients than the trees require, causing them to heavily depend on the biotic community of the forest, particularly the efficient recycling of dead trees. Redwood forests provide habitat for various reptiles, birds, amphibians, and mammals, and old-growth redwoods provide breeding habitat for the endangered Marbled Murrelet and the threatened Spotted Owl.

INTERESTING FACTS

• *Sequoia sempervirens* are among the oldest living things on Earth, the oldest recorded at around 2,200 years old.

• The trees have adapted a response to forest fires, including an extremely thick bark and lack of flammable resin or pitch within the wood.

• Many coast redwoods were lost in a frenzy of logging lasting over a century, particularly around 1850 as the demand for mine and building timber created by the California gold rush increased.

• Opposition to redwood logging began in 1900 resulting in the establishment of the Sempervirens Club, the first activist organization to formally work to preserve the trees.

HABITAT AND DISTRIBUTION

Habitat
Coast redwoods typically grow in the mountains, where moisture from the ocean creates greater precipitation. The oldest and tallest trees can be found in deep gullies and valleys where streams flow year-round and moisture from fog is regular. The trees are naturally protected from loggers as the terrain makes it difficult to access the trees and remove them after felling. The common elevation range for these trees is 100–2,460 ft (30–750 m), but can extend down to sea level or up to 3,000 ft (900 m).

Distribution
Coast redwoods can be found in a narrow strip of land along the Pacific coast, from southwest Oregon to Monterey County, California; the covered land is approximately 40 mi (50 km) long, ranging from 5 to 47 mi (8–75 km) in width. The northern boundary is on the Chetco River on the western edge of the Klamath Mountains near the California-Oregon border; the southern boundary is the Los Padres National Forest's Silver Peak Wilderness in the Santa Lucia Mountains of the Big Sur area.

Cones: Seed cones are ovoid, reaching 0.56–1.25 in (15–32 mm) in length with 15–25 scales spirally arranged. Each cone scale bears 3–7 seeds, which are 3–4 mm long and 0.5 mm broad with two wings 1 mm wide. Pollen cones are ovular and 4–6 mm long.

GIANT REDWOOD
Sequoiadendron giganteum

Avg height: 250–280 ft (76–85 m)
Avg trunk diameter: 15–26 ft (5–8 m)
Lifespan: 750–3,000 years

Bark: The bark is furrowed and fibrous. The bark will grow very thick particularly toward the base of the trunk, reaching up to 3 ft (90 cm) thick. As its name suggests, the bark is reddish-brown in color.

Foliage: The leaves of the giant redwood are awl-shaped, persistent, sessile, and evergreen, reaching 3–6 mm in length. The leaves are arranged spirally on the shoots and range from a dark green to light green color, lightening at the ends of the shoots.

Cones: Although seed cones mature after 18–20 months, they often remain closed and green in color for up to 20 years. They reach 1.5–3 in (4–7 cm) in length and have 30–50 scales per cone with several seeds on each scale, which are arranged spirally.

Sequoiadendron giganteum, also known as giant sequoia, giant redwood, Sierra redwood, or Wellingtonia, are the most massive trees on Earth. They are the sole living species in the Sequoiadendron genus and one of only three species of coniferous tree known as redwoods. There are fewer than 80,000 of these trees remaining and the species is listed as endangered by the IUCN. In many ways, giant redwoods are adapted to forest fires and depend on them for regeneration; their cones typically open after a fire and their thick bark is particularly fire resistant. Without fire clearing the undergrowth, shade-loving plants will crowd out sequoia seedlings and prevent their germination. While these trees are naturally very fire resistant, the dramatic increase in forest fires in recent years as a result of climate change has greatly affected these trees.

INTERESTING FACTS

• Giant redwoods are some of the oldest living organisms on Earth, with the oldest known specimen recorded between 3,200–3,275 years old based on dendrochronology.

• In 2020, the California lightning wildfire called the Castle Fire is thought to have wiped out 10–14% of the giant redwood population, between 7,500–10,600 mature trees.

• The tallest giant redwood can be found in the Redwood Mountain Grove, which is the largest grove of giant sequoia trees on Earth, located in both Kings Canyon National Park and Giant Sequoia National Monument. The tree is measured at 311 ft (95 m) tall.

HABITAT AND DISTRIBUTION

Habitat
The giant sequoia is most commonly found in humid climates that have snowy winters and dry summers. In the south, the groves are typically at an elevation of 5,580–7,050 ft (1,700–2,150 m) while in the north, the elevation of the groves ranges from 4,600 to 6,600 ft (1,400–2,000 m). On northern mountains, the groves typically occur on the south-facing sides, while on more southerly slopes, groves occur on the northern faces.

Distribution
Natural distribution is limited to a small area of the western Sierra Nevada in California. Many of these trees are protected in Giant Sequoia National Monument and Kings Canyon and Sequoia National Parks. There are a total of 77 groves of giant sequoias, which occur exclusively in scattered groves, rather than pure stands. The total area that is claimed by these trees is only 35,620 acres (144.16 km²) with groves ranging from small groves containing as few as 6 trees to areas containing 20,000 mature trees.

Avg height: 210–230 ft (64–70 m)
Avg trunk diameter: 10–23 ft (3–7 m)
Lifespan: Up to 400 yrs

Bark: The bark is thin and fibrous with a stringy texture. Shallow ridges and narrow furrows create a vertical, interwoven pattern. The bark peels away in long, thin strips.

Buttress and knees: Bald cypresses that grow in swampy and flood-prone areas are believed to grow buttresses to provide structural support

Foliage: Needles are yellowish-green in spring and summer, reaching 0.25–0.75 in (1.3–1.9 cm) in length. They appear lacy, being flat, soft, and feathery, and grow in ranks of two. In the fall, they turn cinnamon-brown or orange.

Cones: Young female cones are purple-green, maturing to brown. They reach 1 in (2.5 cm) in diameter and are rounded and wrinkled with 20–40 spirally arranged, four-sided scales per cone. Male cones emerge on panicles near the edge of branchlets

BALD CYPRESS
Taxodium distichum

The bald cypress, also called the red cypress, tidewater red cypress, gulf cypress, white cypress, and swamp cypress, is a pyramidal conifer that, while it resembles a needled evergreen in summer, is actually deciduous. This is the origin of its common name, "bald". In the deep south, the tree can be found growing directly in swampy water often in large stands; trunks often develop root growths called "cypress knees" that protrude above the water surface around the tree. The trunks are buttressed at the base, typically single and straight, and the wood is inherently rot-resistant. As a result, the wood was often used for heavy construction including bridges, boats, warehouses, and docks, as well as interior trim and general millwork. In 1963, the bald cypress was officially designated as the state tree of Louisiana.

INTERESTING FACTS

• The seeds of *Taxodium distichum* are the largest of any species of *Cupressaceae*, reaching 5–10 mm) in length.

• The tallest known specimen is located near Williamsburg, Virginia. It is measured at 145 ft (44.11 m) tall. The stoutest, which is in the Real County near Leakey, Texas, has a trunk diameter of 12.4 ft (3.8 m).

• The largest bald cypress, listed on the National Register of Champion Trees by American Forest, is the National Champion Bald Cypress, in the Cat Island National Wildlife Refuge near St. Francisville, Louisiana. It is 96 ft (29 m) tall with a circumference of 56 ft (17 m), and estimated to be 1,500 years old.

HABITAT AND DISTRIBUTION

Habitat
Taxodium distichum grows in southern rivers, bayous, and swamps. The tree grows well in full sun to partial shade, and in medium to wet, moisture-retentive but reasonably well-drained soils. While it prefers sandy, acidic, moist soils, it will tolerate a wide range including wet soils in standing water to relatively dry soils. The tree prefers humid climates where annual rainfall ranges from 30–64 in (760–1,630 mm) ranging from west to east. Lower temperatures and humidity are best tolerated by larger trees.

Distribution
The bald cypress is primarily found in coastal areas of the southeast from Texas to Maryland and from the southeast corner of Missouri south to the lower Mississippi River valley. The native range extends from the Mississippi River to southeastern Oklahoma and east Texas, east to Florida and north to southeastern New Jersey. The largest remaining old-growth stands of the bald cypress can be found at Corkscrew Swamp Sanctuary near Naples, Florida, and in the Three Sisters track near the Black River in eastern North Carolina.

HARDWOOD TREES

JOSHUA TREE
Yucca brevifolia

Avg height: 15–30 ft (4.5–9 m)
Avg trunk diameter: 12–36 in (30.5–91.5 cm)
Lifespan: 100–200 years

Yucca brevifolia, also known as Joshua tree, palm tree yucca, tree yucca, and yucca palm, is a monocotyledonous tree, meaning it is a grasslike flowering plant. While it grows to tree size, it behaves like a yucca plant in every other aspect. The trunk lacks annual growth rings and consists of thousands of small fibers. The tree has an extensive and deep root system and a top-heavy branch system. The trunk base of a mature tree is enlarged and can reach almost 4 feet (1.2 m) in diameter. While the trunk is relatively wide, it only extends around 1 foot (0.3 m) into the ground and depends mainly on its roots and rhizomes for support. The branches are stout and form an open, rounded canopy. The Joshua tree is used as nesting sites for around 25 species of birds and the seeds are a food source for a small number of mammals.

INTERESTING FACTS

• The common name "Joshua tree" is said to have been given by a group of Mormon settlers in the mid-19th century as the trees guided them in their journey across the Mojave Desert.

• *Yucca brevifolia* is pollinated exclusively by the yucca moth, which has tentacle-like fronds that they use to collect and distribute pollen from the tree's flowers. In turn, the seeds of the Joshua tree fruit is the only food source for the yucca moth caterpillars, which hatch on the flowers' seeds.

• While the lack of annual growth rings make age estimation a challenge, there are specimens that are recorded to be between 500–1,000 years old.

Bark: The bark of the Joshua tree is thick and scaly. It is mostly covered by a mass of small fibers.

Flowers: The flowers are comprised of clusters 12–22 in (30–55 cm) tall and 12–15 in (30–38 cm) broad, the individual flowers erect, 1.5–2.75 in (4–7 cm) tall, with six creamy white to green tepals.

HABITAT AND DISTRIBUTION

Habitat
The range of the Joshua tree has been predicted to be reduced and shifted as a result of climate change, with particular concern being that they will be eliminated from Joshua Tree National Park altogether. Their natural habitat mostly coincides with the geographical reach of the Mojave Desert and is one of the major indicator species for the area. The species is found between 1,300–5,900 ft (400–1,800 m) elevation. The tree is drought tolerant and grows easily in dry, coarse, well-drained soils in full sun.

Distribution
The Joshua tree is found in the southwest, specifically Nevada, Utah, Arizona, and California. It is mostly confined to the Mojave Desert and is particularly prosperous in the grasslands of Lost Horse Valley and Queen Valley, found in Joshua Tree National Park in California. Other areas that host large populations of the tree include the area along US 93 between the towns of Wikieup and Wickenburg in Arizona, and northeast of Kingman, Arizona, in Mohave County.

Fruit: The semifleshy fruit that is produced is green-brown, elliptical, and contains many flat seeds.

BIGLEAF MAPLE
Acer macrophyllum

Avg height: 50–65 ft (15–20 m)
Avg trunk diameter: 24–48 in (61–122 cm)
Lifespan: 50–200 years

Bark: The bark is thin, rarely developing to more than 0.5 in (1.3 cm) thick. When young, the bark is grayish-brown in color and smooth; as the tree ages, the bark becomes a dark brown color and is deeply furrowed with interlacing ridges.

Foliage: The largest of any maple, the leaves reach 5.9–11.8 in (15–30 cm) across. The leaves have five palmate lobes that are deeply incised, the largest running up to 24 in (61 cm). In the spring and summer the leaves transition from burgundy to glossy or deep green; in fall, they turn yellow and gold before falling.

Flowers and fruit: The bigleaf maple produces flowers in spring, with greenish-yellow petals that reach 4–6 in (10–15 cm) in length. The flowers precede the leaves. After 10 years or so, the bigleaf maple begins producing seeds, which are contained in fruit, which is a paired winged samara. Each seed is around 0.38–0.63 in (1–1.5 cm) in diameter with a wing that reaches 1.63–2 in (4–5 cm).

Acer macrophyllum or the bigleaf maple, and commonly known as Oregon maple, has the largest leaves of any maple. It is particularly abundant in mixed-evergreen forests, creating a stunning backdrop when the maple's leaves turn gold in the fall. Considered to be the largest species of maple in North America, the trees are usually as wide-spreading as they are tall. Those that grow in full sun develop broad, rounded crowns with branches that grow low to the ground, while shaded trees develop crowns that are narrow pyramidal in form and trunks clear of branches for half or two thirds of their height. Sap from the bigleaf maple can be used to make maple syrup, but as the concentration of sugar in its sap is much lower than other maples a larger amount is needed to make the same quantity of syrup.

INTERESTING FACTS

• The wood of the bigleaf maple is used for a diverse range of applications including salad bowls, piano frames, and furniture. It is also used for gun stocks, guitar bodies, stringed instruments, and veneer. It is the only commercially important maple of the Pacific Coast region.

• The largest bigleaf maple can be found in Lane County, Oregon. It stands at 119 ft (36 m) tall with a trunk diameter of 12.3 ft (3.7 m) and a crown spread of 91 ft (28 m).

• The bigleaf maple supports more mosses and other plant life than any other tree in the region.

HABITAT AND DISTRIBUTION

Habitat
The bigleaf maple grows predominantly in mountainous regions, preferring moist woods, forests, and canyons. In moist soils with close proximity to streams, bigleaf maples can form pure stands. More often than not, however, they are found within riparian hardwood forests, within open canopies of conifers or mixed forests of oaks or evergreens. The tree is a dominant species in mixed woods that are cool and moist.

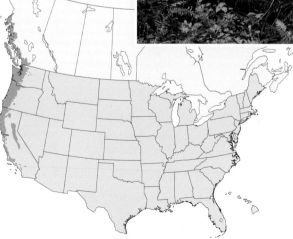

Distribution
Acer macrophyllum can be found in western North America mostly near the Pacific coast from southernmost Alaska to southern California. Additional stands can be found in the foothills of the Sierra Nevada mountains of central California as well as a small population in central Idaho. It is widespread in the foothills of the Cascade Region, the Klamath-Siskiyou Mountains, and the Coast Ranges, and its best development is in southern Oregon.

BOXELDER MAPLE
Acer negundo

Avg height: 35–80 ft (10–25 m)
Avg trunk diameter: 12–20 in (30–50 cm)
Lifespan: 40–60 years

Bark: The bark is a light brown or pale gray and is furrowed into broad, interlacing ridges with deep clefts. Young bark is often warty.

Foliage: The boxelder maple is unusual in that its leaves are pinnately compound with 3–7 leaflets. These leaflets are 1.25–2.75 in (3–7 cm) wide and 2–4 in (5–10 cm) long with slightly serrated margins. When they are in groups of three, the leaflets are often mistaken for poison ivy. In spring and summer they are a translucent light green while in fall turn yellow.

Flowers: Yellow-green flowers appear in early spring. Pistillate flowers grow on drooping racemes, reaching 4–8 in (10–20 cm) in length, while staminate flowers grow in clusters on pedicels. Boxelder maples are fully dioecious; so both male and female trees are required for reproduction. Each seed is 0.5–0.75 in (1–2 cm) long, encased in paired incurved samaras 0.75–1.25 in (2–3 cm) in length that drop in autumn or may persist through the winter.

Acer negundo, the boxelder maple is familiar to people over a large geographic range, so it has numerous common names, including box elder, boxelder maple, Manitoba maple, ash-leaf maple, cut-leaved maple, three-leaf maple, ash maple, sugar maple, negundo maple, and river maple. The tree often has several trunks and can grow to form impenetrable thickets. It is a fast-growing and relatively short-lived tree, typically reaching 60 years or occasionally up to 100 in particularly favorable conditions. In some areas it is considered a weedy species and it can colonize cultivated and uncultivated areas very quickly. Due to its rapid growth, it is a popular tree for use in landscaping, in spite of its vulnerability to storm damage and general poor form. Its crown is generally irregular and rounded.

INTERESTING FACTS

• *Acer negundo* is fully dioecious. The pistillate and staminate flowers are on different trees, so the seeds develop and are enclosed by the samara fruit only the female tree.

• Native Americans used the wood for a variety of purposes including burning in an altar fire during peyote ceremonies, burning the wood for charcoal for ceremonial painting and tattooing, and making prayer sticks, pipe stems, drums, dishes, bowls, and tubes for bellows.

• The oldest extant wood flutes, excavated by Earl H. Morris in 1931 in northeastern Arizona, are dated to 620–670 CE and are made from *Acer negundo* wood.

HABITAT AND DISTRIBUTION

Habitat
Preferring bright sunlight, the boxelder maple often grows in disturbed areas with ample water supply such as riparian habitats and flood plains. It is tolerant of a wide range of soils including relatively dry soils, but is intolerant of shade. As it is a fast-growing tree, it is easily damaged by winds although it is resistant to drought and cold.

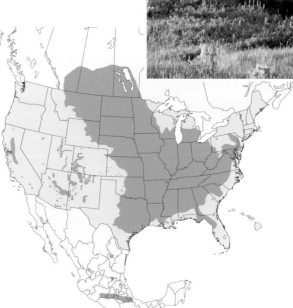

Distribution
The boxelder maple is very widely distributed, having the greatest range of all the maples. It extends from Canada to Guatemala and from coast to coast; it is found from central Florida to New York, west to southern Texas, northwest through the Plains region to northwestern Montana. There are also groups of stands in the central and southern Rocky Mountains and Colorado Plateau, typically along watercourses. In California, it grows on the western slopes of the San Bernardino Mountains, the interior valleys of the Coast range, and the Central Valley along the Sacramento and San Joaquin Rivers.

RED MAPLE
Acer rubrum

Avg height: 120 ft (18–36 m)
Avg trunk diameter: 18–35 in (46–88 cm)
Lifespan: 60–100 years

Bark: On a young tree, the bark is smooth and pale gray. As the tree grows, the bark turns light brown or gray and is furrowed into broad, scaly ridges with deep clefts.

Foliage: The leaves typically have three principal triangular lobes, occasionally five with the two lower lobes being largely suppressed. The leaves reach 2–5 in (5–12.7 cm) long and have toothed edges and pointed tips.

Flowers: Red with five small petals appear before the leaves in late winter to early spring. Staminate flowers are sessile. Pistillate flowers grow on pedicels that lengthen to 0.5–2 in (1–5 cm) long while flowers are blooming, so they hang in clusters.

Fruit: The two-winged samara reaches 0.6–1 in (1.5–2.5 cm) in length with the wings growing at an angle of 50–60 degrees.

Acer rubrum, commonly called red maple, swamp maple, water maple, and soft maple, is a medium-sized tree with a rounded to oval crown. The epithet of *rubrum*, meaning red, is evident in its red flowers that grow in dense clusters in late March to early April; its red samaras; its reddish twigs, stems, and buds; and in fall, its spectacular orange-red foliage. It is one of the most common and widespread deciduous trees of central and eastern North America and is recognized by the U.S. Forest Service as the most abundant native tree in eastern North America. While it is often used in landscaping as a shade tree, it is also considered weedy or invasive in certain areas, particularly young or frequently logged forests. Its root networks are fibrous and dense, preventing other plants from growing near its trunk.

INTERESTING FACTS

• The leaves of red maple are extremely toxic to horses, particularly when wilted or dead. The actual toxin is unknown but is believed to be an oxidant as it damages red blood cells.

• While red maples don't live very long by tree standards, they start producing seeds after only four years.

• Because the wood of the red maple is relatively soft and often deformed, it is rarely used for lumber. It is more commonly used to produce smaller items such as hangers, clothespins, wooden boxes, and musical instruments. More uniform wood is used for flooring and furniture.

HABITAT AND DISTRIBUTION

Habitat
The red maple grows best in full sun to partial shade and medium to wet soils. It is particularly tolerant of wet soil and is very cold hardy. In southern states, the tree often occurs in rocky upland areas that tend to be drier, while in northern states it usually occurs in wet woods, river floodplains, or wet bottomland. It grows well at elevations between sea level and 3,000 ft (900 m).

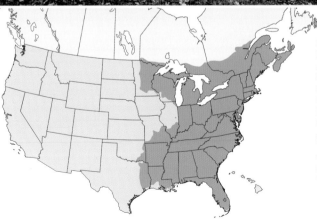

Distribution
Native to central and eastern North America, the red maple extends from Quebec and Minnesota south to eastern Texas and the southern tip of Florida. Of any tree that occurs in Florida, it has the largest continuous range along the North American Atlantic Coast. In total, it ranges over 1,600 mi (2,600 km) from north to south. In the extreme west of its range and the southeast it is rare but can be found in specific habitats.

SILVER MAPLE
Acer saccharinum

Avg height: 50–80 ft (15–25 m)
Avg trunk diameter: 36–60 in (91–152 cm)
Lifespan: 80–130 years

Bark: On young trees, the bark is smooth and silvery. Over time, the bark darkens to gray to brown-gray in color. As the tree matures, the trunk and limbs develop a shaggy appearance as the bark develops into long, flaky scales which lift away from the trunk over time.

Foliage: Leaves are a greenish-yellow color in spring and summer. In fall they are typically a pale yellow, occasionally bright yellow or orange. The underside of the leaves are a silvery color, giving the tree its common name. The leaves have five lobes with deep angular notches between. The leaves reach 2.25–4.75 in (6–12 cm) wide and 3.25–6.25 in (8–16 cm) long with long, slender stalks reaching 2–4.75 in (5–12 cm) in length.

Flowers and fruit: In early spring, greenish-yellow flowers bloom in dense clusters, preceding the foliage. The flowers are followed by paired samaras that mature in late spring, which grow to around 1.25–2 in (3–5 cm) in length. Each samara contains a single small seed, around 5–10 mm in diameter. The samaras are among the largest fruits of a maple tree within the tree's range.

Acer saccharinum, also known as silver maple, white maple, swamp maple, water maple, large maple, soft maple, silverleaf maple, or creek maple, gets its name from the silvery underside of its leaves. It is a medium to tall tree with a rounded open-spreading crown. It is fast-growing and was very popular in landscaping for urban areas; however, its shallow root systems can damage sidewalks. As with all fast-growing trees, however, the wood is weak and can be easily damaged in high winds or when coated with ice or snow in winter. While the epithet saccharinum means "sweet" and the sap can be used to make maple syrup, its sugar concentration is greatly inferior to the sap of the sugar maple. The wood is often turned into pulp to make paper, while lumber is used to make tool handles, crates, musical instruments, flooring, and furniture, as the wood is light and easily worked.

INTERESTING FACTS

• The silver maple and its cousin the red maple are the only *Acer* species to produce their samaras fruit crop in spring rather than fall.

• The large rounded buds are one of the primary food sources for squirrels, chipmunks, and birds during the spring in the eastern U.S. after nuts and acorns have sprouted and food is scarce. The bark is eaten by deer and beavers.

• Native Americans used the bark of the silver maple for medicinal purposes. The Cherokee take an infusion of the bark for hives, dysentery, and cramps and boil the inner bark to use as a wash for sore eyes. A bark infusion from the south side of the tree is used by the Mohegan for cough medicine.

HABITAT AND DISTRIBUTION

Habitat
Preferring medium to wet soils, the silver maple grows best in full sun to partial shade. Tolerant of both drought and wet soil, it is easily grown in a range of conditions. It typically occurs in moist to wet and often poorly drained soils on floodplains, along the edges of rivers and streams, and in low woods. Its tendency to grow in wetlands and along waterways lead to the colloquial name "water maple."

Distribution
The silver maple is native to eastern North America and is commonly found. The natural range extends to the Midwest and southern Ontario and southwestern Quebec. It is not found in the humid Atlantic or Gulf coastal plains south of Maryland but is confined to the Appalachians and inland,

SUGAR MAPLE
Acer saccharum

Avg height: 80–115 ft (25–35 m)
Avg trunk diameter: 30–36 in (76–91 cm)
Lifespan: 200–400 years

Bark: The bark of a young tree is light gray and smooth. As the tree ages, the bark turns a gray-brown and becomes rough and deeply furrowed. The bark takes on a shaggy appearance over time as it lifts away from the trunk. The long, thick irregular plates curl outward, creating firm ridges.

Foliage: The leaves are medium in size, around 3–8 in (7.6–20.3 cm) long and wide and with 3–5 lobes. In spring and fall they are a light to dark green, turning yellow-orange in fall with occasional color variations. The color range is spectacular and can include fluorescent red-orange and bright yellow, often coloring unevenly.

Flowers and fruit: The male and female flowers fall together, each on separate long tendrils but from the same panicles, in groups of 8 to 14. They are yellow-green in color and lack petals. The fruit of the sugar maple is the two-winged samara, which develops in the summer and falls in autumn. The seeds are globose, 7–10 mm in diameter, and the samara averages 1 in (2.5 cm) in length.

Acer saccharum, also known as the sugar maple, sweet maple, curly maple, birds-eye maple, or rock maple, is a main component of the eastern U.S. hardwood forest, and its dense, rounded crown is one of the main trees responsible for giving New England its reputation for stunning fall foliage. Native Americans taught the colonists how to tap the trees to extract the sap and boil it down to create maple syrup, and this is now a major industry for both large and small farms. The development of sap is dependent on cold weather, so the collection of sap for sugar is not possible in the tree's southern range as the winter temperatures aren't cold enough. The wood is heavy and durable, making it well suited for many uses including musical instruments, sporting goods, furniture, and veneer.

INTERESTING FACTS

- While the sugar content in the sap is much higher than that of other maples, it takes 40 gallons of sap to produce 1 gallon of maple syrup. Each tree yields between 5 and 60 gallons of sap per year.

- The wood of the sugar maple is often used to make bowling pins and bowling alleys, as well as basketball courts including the floors used by the NBA, and pool cues.

- The sugar maple is depicted on the state quarter of Vermont and is the state tree of Wisconsin, West Virginia, Vermont, and New York.

HABITAT AND DISTRIBUTION

Habitat
The sugar maple is tolerate of heavy shade, although it grows best in full sun to part shade. It is easily grown in soil that is average, medium moisture, and well-drained, but it grows best in fertile, slightly acidic, moist soils. It is intolerant of compacted or poorly drained soils and is particularly affected by road salt and urban pollution. Pure stands are very common and are a major component of hardwood forests in the north and midwest.

Distribution
The sugar maple is native to the hardwood forests of eastern Canada and to northeastern and northcentral U.S. From Nova Scotia, New Brunswick and southern Ontario and Manitoba, the range extends south from Minnesota through Missouri in the west and from Maine to Tennessee in the east. South of Maryland, it is principally in the Appalachian Mountains. There are pockets of these trees in North Carolina, western South Carolina, northern Georgia, northeastern South Dakota, and southwestern Oklahoma.

MAPLES

Of the 132 species of maples around the Northern Hemisphere (only one is found south of the Equator), all but the Boxelder have lobed, palmate leaves: instead of a single main vein from which all the others branch off, there may be up to five main veins in the lobed leaf. In fall, many maples are brilliantly colored in shades of bright yellow, orange, or red. All maples produce fruits known as samuras, or maple keys, carrying pairs of seeds encased in papery wings that are dispersed by the wind. Most maples have both male and female flowers on the same tree (monoecious). However, the Boxelder is entirely dioecious, with flowers of just one sex on any tree so it must have a female tree and a male tree in order to reproduce. The Silver and Red Maples may switch between being dioecious and monoecious and, also, between being only male or only female. The Bigleaf Maple has hermaphroditic flowers: both male and female parts on the same flower.

Bigleaf Maple *Acer macrophyllum*

The leaves are the biggest of any maple, up to 12 inches wide.

The leaves are gold to yellow in the fall.

The blossoms are hermaphroditic: both male and female come out of the same stem. The petals are inconspicuous.

The samaras are attached at an acute angle.

Boxelder *Acer negundo*

The only maple with pinnately compound leaves; "leaves of three," which are sometimes mistaken for poison ivy.

The leaves are yellow in the fall.

male flowers

female flowers

The samaras are green in summer and have an incurved wing.

Red Maple *Acer rubrum*

Most leaves have three lobes. The top is light green; the bottom is whitish and waxy or hairy.

The fall leaves are usually a bright red.

male flowers   female flowers

The samaras range in color from light brown to reddish, and ripen in the spring.

Silver Maple *Acer saccharinum*

The leaves have deep angular notches between the lobes and downy silver undersides

In fall, leaves are yellow or, rarely, orange or red.

The yellow male flowers and the red female flowers come out before the leaves

The samaras, which are larger than those of any other maple in North America, ripen in the spring.

Sugar Maple *Acer saccharum*

The leaves have deep, rounded notches.

Sugar Maples are known for their brilliant fall foliage of yellow, orange, red.

Both male and female flowers fall on long tendrils from the same panicles.

Especially globose seeds, in samaras that turn brown while the seeds are still green

Avg height: 25–60 ft (7.6–18.3 m)
Avg trunk diameter: 20–40 in (50.8–101.6 cm)
Lifespan: 150–200 years

Bark: The bark is a light gray color, roughened by small lumps, and may be splotchy in color. The trunk has small protrusions of wood which gives the bark its knotted look. The bark is overall smooth regardless of age or size. The bark is quite thin and is easily removed.

Foliage: The leaves are thick, smooth, and leathery with spiny marginal teeth. They are a deep green in color and are around 0.8–1.6 in (2–4 cm) wide and 2–4 in (5–10 cm) long. The leaves are oval in shape and taper to a very sharp point. Male and female flowers in each raceme. The flowers appear in early spring, before the leaves

Flowers and fruit: Blossoms are small and a greenish or creamy white color that grow in small clusters and bloom in May through June. The holly fruit is showy, the bright orange or red berries reaching 6–12 mm in diameter, each containing four seeds. The fruit ripens in the fall on pollinated female trees and persists, bearing seed at about ten years of age.

AMERICAN HOLLY
Ilex opaca

The American holly, also known as American holly, white holly, prickly holly, evergreen holly, Christmas holly, or yule holly, is an evergreen tree that is upright and pyramidal. It is easily identified due to its distinctive spiny green leaves and bright red berries born on stout, stiff branches. It is commonly used for Christmas decorations and the berry-laden boughs are often collected at Christmas time each year. The brightly colored berries are a favorite food source for birds in winter when other food sources are scarce, although the berries are poisonous to humans, cats, and dogs. Both male and female trees are required for berries to develop. The fine-textured whitish wood is used for inlays in rulers, carvings, handles, and cabinetwork and takes stains very well; it is often dyed and used in place of ebony.

INTERESTING FACTS

- The American holly was named the state tree of Delaware on May 1, 1939.
- The European holly is very similar to the American holly. The main differences are the leaves of the European holly are brighter than those of the American, and the European tree is smaller in overall size.
- The American holly is the only member of the holly family that can grow to tree size.

HABITAT AND DISTRIBUTION

Habitat
The American holly is most commonly found in swamp peripheries, forest bottomlands, and moist woods, and occasionally coastal dunes. The tree grows best in consistently moist, average, acidic, well-drained soils in partial shade to full sun. When growing in more alkaline soils, the leaves turn yellow. While the holly tolerates a wide range of soil conditions, it will not tolerate soil that is too saturated with moisture from flooding.

Distribution
Native to central and eastern U.S., the American holly ranges from eastern Texas to central Florida, north to southeastern Missouri, Ohio, West Virginia, and Massachusetts. In the northernmost part of its range, it is found in sparse numbers from southern Connecticut, southeastern New York, northern New Jersey, north to Cape Cod, Massachusetts. Further south in the lowlands of the Gulf and Atlantic, the tree is abundant.

BLACK MANGROVE
Avicennia germinans

Avg height: 30–50 ft (9.1–15.2 m)
Avg trunk diameter: 12–24 in (30.5–61 cm)
Lifespan: 60–100 years

Bark: When the tree is young, the bark is smooth and a dark gray color. As the tree ages, the bark becomes scaly, thick, and fissured as the trunk increases in size. The bark of a mature tree is a very dark brown, almost black color, which gives the tree its name "black mangrove."

Foliage: Leaves are evergreen, elliptic, and thick. They are dark green above and pale gray and hairy below. The topsides of the leaves often appear white due to the deposits of salt that are excreted from the leaves. The leaves reach 1.5–2.5 in (3.8–6.4 cm) in length.

Flowers and fruit: The tree bears small, white flowers with dark-spotted corollas and yellow centers. The seeds germinate in midsummer but can be found on the tree year-round and can remain viable for a year once released. The seeds are encased in a fruit, which reveals the seedling when it falls into the water. The fruits resemble large flattened capsules that come to a point.

Avicennia germinans or the black mangrove is an evergreen shrub or small to medium-sized tree. It has spreading branches with a rounded crown, supported by a trunk that is often crooked. It is found in the southeast U.S., where it thrives on muddy and sandy shores reached by seawater. Unlike other mangrove species, the black mangrove does not grow aerial roots but rather possesses pneumatophores, vertical roots that allow it to breathe when fully submerged in water. The tree is hardy and is able to expel salt that it has absorbed through the roots from its leaves, giving them a whitish appearance. The black mangrove often grows in proximity to the red and white mangrove trees and together, the three trees stabilize the shoreline and provide buffers from storm surges.

INTERESTING FACTS

- Because the wood has an interlocked grain, it is difficult to work with and difficult to finish due to its oily texture. It is often used for posts, pilings, fuel, and charcoal.
- The bark of the black mangrove has been used as a black dye and in the process of tanning animal skins.
- The flowers are an important source of "mangrove honey," which is a clear whitish color of high quality, as the trees are one of the few saltwater plants bees will forage nectar from.
- Black mangroves provide nursery grounds, breeding, and feeding for a wide variety of birds, shellfish, fish, and other wildlife.

HABITAT AND DISTRIBUTION

Habitat
Avicennia germinans grows in brackish water estuaries and coastal lagoons, just above the high tide line. Compared to other species of mangroves, it is less tolerant of highly saline conditions. In cooler areas of its range, the black mangrove is considered a small shrub. The black mangrove penetrates farthest inland of all the mangrove species, although it becomes smaller and can be affected by cold winters. The tree grows best in full sun.

Distribution
The black mangrove is native to Florida and is found on coasts and mudflats throughout subtropical and tropical regions of the U. S. Because the black mangrove is a semi-tropical to tropical species, its range is limited by freezing temperatures. The tree's range extends from Texas along the Gulf Coast through Louisiana to the southern tip of Florida.

RED ALDER
Alnus rubra

Avg height: 65–100 ft (19.8–30.5 m)
Avg trunk diameter: 1–3 ft (30.5–91.4 cm)
Lifespan: 80–100 years

Bark: The bark is smooth, thin, and an ashy-gray color, and is often mottled. Because of its whitish appearance, the tree is often confused with paper birch. When damaged, the bark turns bright rust red, giving the tree its common name. The bark is often colonized by moss or white lichen.

Foliage: The leaves, which reach 2.8–5.9 in (7–15 cm) in length, are ovate and come to a point with bluntly serrated edges. Unlike other alders, the ends of the leaves begin to curl under at the edge. In fall, the leaves turn yellow before falling.

Male catkins on left, female cones on right: Male flowers are slim, dangling, cylindrical clusters reaching 3.9–5.9 in (10–15 cm) long and reddish. Fruit develops into superficially conelike oval fruits 0.75–1.5 in (1.9–3.8 cm) long with the seeds developing between the woody bracts of the "cones." The seeds are shed in late fall and winter.

The red alder, sometimes called the Oregon alder, is one of the largest species of alders in the world and the largest in North America. Its name is derived from its bark which, when scraped or bruised, turns a bright rusty red color. It is a deciduous broadleaf tree with a straight trunk supporting spreading branches forming a broadly conical shape. Larger trees often lack branches for a considerable distance from the ground. Red alder is considered to be the most important commercial hardwood of the Pacific Northwest as the wood has a fine, even texture and has moderate density. It is easy to work with and sands and polishes evenly. It stains well, holds paints and coatings, and seldom splits. Also, less expensive than other hardwoods makes it ideal for plywood, veneer, pallets, paneling and trim.

INTERESTING FACTS

• The official tallest red alder can be found in Clatsop County, Oregon, and stands 105 ft (32 m) tall.

• The bark was used by Native Americans to create a russet dye, used to darken fishing nets to make them less visible underwater. Native Americans also used the bark to treat skin irritations, insect bites, and poison oak, as well as tuberculosis and lymphatic disorders.

• Because the wood has an oily smoke when burned, it is a choice option for smoking salmon.

• Red alder is an important source of pulp for paper.

HABITAT AND DISTRIBUTION

Habitat
In the northwestern Coast Ranges and southern Alaska, the red alder grows on moist and cool slopes. At the southern end of its range in California and more inland, it grows predominantly along the edges of wetlands and watercourses. It is tolerant of infertile soil. It commonly grows in wetland-riparians, mixed evergreen forests, redwood forests, and closed-cone pine forests.

Distribution
Native in western North America, the red alder can be found in Montana, Idaho, California, Oregon, Washington, Yukon, and Alaska. The tree almost always grows within about 120 mi (200 km) of the Pacific coast, with the exception of the area across Washington and Oregon into Montana, where it extends up to 370 mi (600 km) inland. There are isolated populations in Idaho and is cultivated in Hawaii.

PAPER BIRCH
Betula papyrifera

Avg height: 50–75 ft (15.2–22.8 m)
Avg trunk diameter: 15–30 in (38.1–76.2 cm)
Lifespan: 30–100 years

Bark: The tree is best identified by its white bark, which peels away from the trunk in papery strips. Older trees develop black markings on the bark. The inner bark is an orange-brown color which shows up in contrast to the white outer bark.

Foliage: Leaves are ovate to triangular, reaching 2–4 in (5–10 cm) in length. The leaves are rounded at the base and taper to a point. They are dark green and smooth above and lighter with slightly hairy veins below. They are irregularly toothed and arranged alternately on the stem.

Flowers and fruit: Male flowers grow in drooping catkins up to 4 in (10 cm) long and are a yellowish-brown color, while female flowers are greenish and grow in upright catkins up to 1.5 in (3.8 cm) in length. The female flowers are followed by fruits that are superficially conelike, each of which contains numerous small winged seeds that mature in late summer.

Paper birch, also known as canoe birch and white birch, is noted for its white bark, which peels away from the trunk in papery strips to reveal the orange-brown inner bark beneath. A tree that has a single straight trunk supports a pyramidal crown aging to an oval rounded crown, while a tree with multiple trunks tends to be shorter with a more irregular crown. In forests, the majority of paper birch trees have a single trunk; When it is grown as a landscape tree it is more likely to develop multiple trunks or branch close to the ground. It is a relatively short-lived species of birch but is often one of the first trees to colonize a burned area. The wood of the paper birch is used for specialty products including toys, broom handles, spools, clothespins, bobbins, toothpicks, and ice cream sticks.

INTERESTING FACTS

• Native Americans made lightweight canoes by stretching paper birch bark over frames made of northern whitecedar, resulting in the common name canoe birch.

• *Betula papyrifera*, being a pioneer species is often the first to grow in areas where plant life has been destroyed by avalanche, wildfire, or high winds. In these conditions, it often forms pure stands.

• The nutritional quality of the bark is poor, but due to its abundance it is a winter staple food for moose. The bark is also eaten by white-tailed deer, the inner bark by beavers and porcupines, and the seeds are eaten by small mammals and birds.

HABITAT AND DISTRIBUTION

Habitat
Paper birch grows best in wet to medium soils and partial shade. It needs consistently moist soils such as well-drained sandy or rocky loams. It grows well in northern climates that are cool and have milder summers and where root zones are covered in snow throughout the winter. It handles humidity and heat poorly and these elements will greatly affect the tree's lifespan. In its northern range, the tree often grows in pure stands or with white or black spruce. In its eastern and central range, it often grows with balsam fir and red spruce, as well as others.

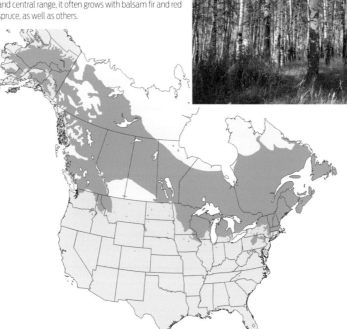

Distribution
Betula papyrifera is predominantly found in the cold climates of Canada and Alaska, with its range extending southward into a few northern states and into the mountains, specifically the Appalachians in North Carolina and the Rockies in Colorado. Isolated stands are also found in Washington, Pennsylvania, and the Hudson Valley in New York. The most southerly found stand in the western region is in Long Canyon in the City of Boulder Open Space and Mountain Parks in Colorado.

Avg height: 20–30 ft (6–9 m)
Avg trunk diameter: 4–8 in (10–20 cm)
Lifespan: 50–150 years

Bark: The bark is thin, fairly smooth, and heavily fluted. It is a bluish-gray color when young, aging to a slate gray. The bark is tight, stretched over an irregularly ridged trunk. As the tree ages, the bark becomes shallowly fissured and even furrowed near the base.

Foliage fruiting branch: The leaves are ovate and alternately arranged with a doubly toothed edge. They are green and yellow in spring and summer, turning a bright golden yellow, orange, or red in fall. Leaves grow to 3–6 in (7.6–15.2 cm) long and 1–3 (2.5–7.6 cm) wide.

AMERICAN HORNBEAM
Carpinus caroliniana

Carpinus caroliniana, commonly known as American hornbeam, ironwood, musclewood, water beech, or blue beech, is a short, stubby tree that can have one or more trunks that are often crooked and fluted. The wood of the American hornbeam is extremely hard, which gives the tree its common name "ironwood." As the tree is relatively small and there is limited wood per tree, however, commercial use of hornbeam wood is restricted to small items such as tool handles, bowls, and walking sticks because it is unlikely to crack. These trees provide good shelter for animals and the inner bark of younger trees is eaten by rabbits and beavers. The buds and seeds are a food source for squirrels, foxes, wild turkeys, quail, ruffed grouse, and a number of songbirds.

INTERESTING FACTS

• The red-spotted purple and eastern tiger swallowtail butterflies rely on these trees as a larval host plant.

• The trunk of the American hornbeam is often coarsely ribbed, resembling a flexed muscle, which in combination with its hard, dense wood gives the tree its common name "muscle wood."

• The largest known American hornbeam can be found in Ulster County, New York. It stands at 69 ft (21 m) tall with a trunk diameter of 30 in (76.2 cm).

HABITAT AND DISTRIBUTION

Habitat
The American hornbeam does best in sandy or clay loams with high organic matter, slightly acidic soils, and regular moisture. Because it tolerates shade well, it is often an understory tree. It is often found near the banks of rivers or streams and is a common understory species of the maritime and riverine forests of eastern temperate states.

Flowers and Fruit: In spring, yellow-green male flowers and fuzzy yellow-green female flowers appear at the same time as the leaves. The male flowers grow in catkins 1–2.5 in (2.5–6.3 cm) long, while the female flowers form 3-lobed bracts 1–1.5 in (2.5–3.8 cm) long, which partially surround the fruit. The fruit is a small ribbed nut that reaches 6–8 mm in length.

Distribution
The native range of the American hornbeam extends from northern Minnesota and northern Michigan east to Maine, south to eastern Texas and central Iowa, and east to central Florida. There are separate populations in Honduras, Guatemala, and central and southern Mexico.

EASTERN HOPHORNBEAM
Ostrya virginiana

Avg height: 20–35 ft (6–10.5 m)
Avg trunk diameter: 8–14 in (20.3–35.5 cm)
Lifespan: 100–150 years

Bark: The bark is thin and gray-brown to brown in color. As the tree grows, the bark splits into narrow vertical strips, which becomes flaky and begins to curl away from the trunk, giving it a distinctive appearance.

Foliage: The leaves are similar to those of a birch. They are oval to lance-shaped, dark yellowish-green in color with sharply serrated edges. They grow 2–5 in (5–13 cm) long and 1.5–2.25 in (4–6 cm) wide. The leaves are smooth above and sparsely to moderately fuzzy below. In fall, they turn a dull yellow and tend to drop early.

Flowers and fruit: The eastern hophornbeam develops male and female catkins, neither of which are particularly showy, with the former reaching 0.75–2 in (2–5 cm) and the latter reaching 0.3–0.6 in (8–15 mm). Male catkins persist throughout the winter, while female catkins are followed by drooping clusters of seed-pairing pods that resemble hops.

Ostrya virginiana, commonly called eastern hophornbeam, American hophornbeam, leverwood, hardhack, or ironwood, is a small to medium-sized understory tree with a generally rounded crown with a spread between 20–30 ft (6–9 m). Its branches are horizontal and drooping. *Ostrya virginiana* is closely related to the American hornbeam (*Carpinus caroliniana*) but differs in that the bark of the former is flaky while the latter's is smooth. The buds and catkins of the hophornbeam are important food sources in winter for ruffed grouse. The nuts are also consumed by downy woodpeckers, rose-breasted grosbeaks, purple finches, ring-necked pheasants, cottontails, gray and red squirrels, and northern bobwhites.

INTERESTING FACTS

• The seeds of *Ostrya virginiana* form in clusters of saclike seed-bearing pods that resemble the fruit of hops (*Humulus lupulus*), which gives the tree its common name.

• It has one of the hardest and toughest woods in its region and was once used for runners on sleighs.

• The American hophornbeam will sprout from its stump even after suffering severe damage from a fire.

HABITAT AND DISTRIBUTION

Habitat
The eastern hophornbeam grows well in medium, average, well-drained soil in partial shade to full sun. It generally occurs in dry soils on bluffs, upland woods, and rocky slopes as an understory tree. The tree is most commonly found at elevations of 2,800–3,200 ft (850–980 m), although it can extend to extremes of 250–750 ft (75–320 m) in Quebec and up to 5,000 ft (1,520 m) in the southern Appalachians.

Distribution
Ostrya virginiana is native to eastern North America and Mexico. The range extends from eastern Wyoming and southern Manitoba east to Nova Scotia and south to the Black Hills of South Dakota. The tree's range includes all eastern states south to eastern Texas and northern Florida.

BIRCHES: LEAVES, BARK, AND FRUITS

Both birches and alders are in the Birch family (Betulaceae), with alternate leaves that are simple, pinnately toothed or serrated. Male and female flowers are borne in separate catkins on the same tree, so all birch trees are monoecious and self-fertilize. The seeds develop in the female catkins, which are generally shorter than those of the male; however, while the fruiting catkins of birches disintegrate as the seeds are dispersed, alder catkins become woody and remain attached to the stems during and for awhile following seed dispersal,

Only the Red Alder (*Alnus rubra*) and the Paper Birch (*Betula papyrifera*) have full profiles but the other alders and birches shown here are also native and widespread in North America, and can be distinguished on the basis of their bark, leaves, and fruit.

Paper Birch *Betula papyrifera*
The white peeling bark makes the Paper Birch the most visually distinctive of the birches; it has double-toothed leaves that are wider at their base and taper toward the top, and short, stout fruiting catkins on long stalks next to male catkins.

Yellow Birch *Betula alleghaniensis*
The bark is yellow-bronze and shiny, and peels in horizontal strips. The doubly serrated leaves are arranged alternately on short stems, and the fruiting catkins are erect.

River Birch *Betula nigra*
The loose layers of bark are curling and paper-thin. The leaves are so deeply toothed that they may appear lobed, and are darker green above and yellower underneath. Unlike other birches, the catkins mature in spring.

Sweet Birch *Betula lenta*
The bark on older trunks has deep vertical cracks and peels in broad plates; the leaves are double toothed; and the catkins are erect rather than pendulous. Perhaps the best way to identify Sweet Birch is not by appearance at all but by the strong wintergreen odor that is released when its twigs or bark are scraped.

Red Alder *Alnus rubra*
The bark is smooth and ashy gray until it is scraped, and the wound turns a deep rusty red, giving the tree its name. Leaves are double-toothed, and the teeth are rounded; unlike all other alders, the outside edges are curled under. Cones persist on the branches for a year or more..

Smooth Alder *Alnus serrulata*
The bark is brownish-gray and smooth. The finely toothed leaves are ovate with the narrower end at the stem, and are smooth on top and hairy on the underside. The cones have short stalks and may be upright.

Speckled Alder *Alnus incana*
The bark has numerous, scattered white pores (lenticels), that are unique among alders. The broad leaves are matte-green in color and coursely double-toothed. The woody cones are hard, dark, and cylindrical, and often can be found hanging near clumps of male catkins.

Green Alder *Alnus alnobetula*
The bark stays smooth and gray as it ages, unusual in alders. The leaves are ovate to rounded with coarse, uneven teeth. Cones are on long slender stems.

Avg height: 30–60 ft (9–18 m)
Avg trunk diameter: 24–48 in (61–122 cm)
Lifespan: 50–75 years

Bark: The southern catalpa has reddish-brown bark that has unevenly shaped shallow fissures. There are visible scales on the bark of the catalpa. Older trees have ridged or plated bark and the younger trees have thin bark that can be easily damaged.

Foliage: The tips of the catalpa tree leaves have short points or are rounded with a heart-shaped base. There are no teeth around the perimeter of the leaves. The leaves are vividly green on top and are lighter on the bottom. The tree sheds its leaves in the winter. When the leaves are bruised, a distinctive odor is emitted.

Flowers and fruit: The cigarlike fruits, usually over 11.8 in (30 cm) long with flat seeds, sometimes remain attached to the tree through the winter. Once mature, the seeds turn from green to dark brown and fall from the fruit after it dries. Thick clusters of trumpetlike white flowers, with shades of orange and purple on the inside, large leaves, give this tree an ornamental look.

SOUTHERN CATALPA
Catalpa bignonioides

Catalpa bignonioides, commonly known as southern catalpa, catalpa, Indian bean tree, or cigartree, was named by Giovanni Antonio Scopoli in 1777. The trunk is thick and short, supporting crooked, straggling branches which form an irregular, broad crown. Catalpas are commonly deciduous trees that have large heart-shaped leaves. They generally grow quickly and saplings will reach half of their mature size in just ten years. White flowers grow in dense panicles, covering the tree so thickly that they almost conceal the leaves.

INTERESTING FACTS

• The appearance of the catalpa leaves is often confused for the leaves of other tree species, including the tung tree and *Paulownia tomentosa*.

• The genus name *Catalpa* is a Native American word, specifically the Muskogean name for the tree.

• *Catalpa bignonioides* is the only food source for the catalpa sphinx moth.

HABITAT AND DISTRIBUTION

Habitat
Ideal conditions for its growth include average, medium to wet and well-drained soil. The southern catalpa can survive regional flooding. It is often found in low woodland, wetlands, and on stream banks.

Distribution
The southern catalpa is native to the southeastern states of the US, including Alabama, Florida, Georgia, Louisiana, and Mississippi. However, over the years, it has become widely grown in areas to which it is not native due to its adaptability.

Avg height: 5–12 ft (1.5–3.6 m)
Avg trunk diameter: 6–12 in (15.25–30.5 cm)
Lifespan: 50–60 years

Bark: The bark of the tree is a light brown color and has a smooth surface texture. As the tree grows older, its bark turns a light grayish brown with corklike bumps and wrinkled bark. Warts may also begin to appear from separated short lenticels along with shallow fissures.

Foliage: The pinnate leaves have 5 to 9 leaflets that are dark green. The leaves can grow to be 1.2–2 in (3–5 cm) long. Each leaflet has serrated margins. The leaves grow in pairs, opposite each other on their respective branches.

Flowers and fruit: The flowers and ripe fruit of the American elderberry are edible and widely popular. The flowers, known as elderflower, are white in color and have an average of 5 flat petals arranged in an umbrella shape with 5 stamens. The flower can grow in broad, flat clusters 5–9 in (12.7–22.8 cm) wide. The fruit is known as the elderberry. It is purplish-black in color and widely used in cooking and the production of cough syrups.

AMERICAN BLACK ELDERBERRY
Sambucus canadensis

A deciduous suckering shrub or small tree, *Sambucus canadensis*, commonly known as American black elderberry, black elder, common elder, Canada elderberry, or common elderberry, has long, arching stems forming a thin, rounded crown. It produces white, lemon-scented flowers in broad, flat clusters and bunches of black elderberry fruits. The genus name *Sambucus* comes from the Greek "sambuce," which is an ancient musical instrument. This refers to the soft pith of the tree's twigs, which is used to make whistles and flutes. The American elder is widely known for its aesthetic flowers and elderberries, which are edible when they ripen.

INTERESTING FACTS

• The twigs and fruit are used to create dyes for basketry.

• While the berries are edible, many parts of the plant contain cyanogenic glycosides and alkaloids, which make them toxic and even lethal at high doses.

• Elderberries are used to make jellies, pies, juice, and wine.

HABITAT AND DISTRIBUTION

Habitat
The American elder requires medium to wet and well-drained soil. It can adapt to moist, loamy, and rich soils, but requires moist soil for ideal growth. Full sun and partial shade are needed, with at least 4 hours of direct sunlight every day. It is often found in drier old fields, ditches, bogs, alluvial forests, and at the edges of riparian thickets.

Distribution
The native distribution of the American elder is a large area of North America east of the Rocky Mountains, as well as Venezuela, and Brazil. It is widely found all across the U.S. and in Canada.

BUTTONWOOD
Conocarpus erectus

Avg height: 20–60 ft (6–18 m)
Avg trunk diameter: 18–40 in (45–100 cm)
Lifespan: 10–20 years

Bark: The bark of the buttonwood is quite thick with broad plates of narrow scales. It is gray to brown in color and has brittle twigs that are angled. With age, the bark of the tree twists.

Foliage: The leaves have an alternate arrangement. They are oblong in shape and can grow to be 0.8–2.75 in (2–7 cm) long and 0.4–1.2 in (1–3 cm) wide. Each leaf has a tapered tip and a smooth margin. The leaves are dark green in colot and have a shine to them, with pale, thin silky hair and two salt glands at their base.

Flowers and fruit: The fruit of the buttonwood looks like buttons, which is the source of its common name. They do not have petals and grow in dense panicles, composed of 35–56 flowers. The fruit, which is 0.2–0.3 in (5–8 mm) in diameter, can be red to brown in color and has conelike seeds, growing to 0.2–0.6 in (5–15 mm) in length.

Conocarpus erectus, also known as buttonwood or button mangrove, is an evergreen mangrove shrub or tree that grows in tropical regions across the globe—from Florida to the Caribbean and extending to Africa and Polynesia. It is a highly dense tree that has multiple trunks. It has proven to be an ideal tree for coastal planting and is often grown as a frontline tree, a shade tree, or a hedge. It has a moderately dense, symmetrical crown that is vase-shaped and spreading, with branches starting to develop low on the trunk.

INTERESTING FACTS

• It is a host plant for the larva of the martial scrub hairstreak butterfly and the tantalus sphinx moth, and is a source of nectar for others.

• The dense wood is often used to make charcoal and as firewood, as it burns slowly and produces a lot of heat, making it a good choice for smoking fish and meats.

• It became the most abundantly planted tree in Kuwait because it was widely used for landscaping.

• The largest buttonwood in the U.S. is 35 ft (11 m) tall with a spread of 70 ft (21 m).

HABITAT AND DISTRIBUTION

Habitat
Ideally, the buttonwood prefers complete sun, high alkaline soil, and salty air because of its tolerance to high salt wind and saltwater. This tree has high drought tolerance as well. It is a hardy plant, growing well in a variety of soils, but is commonly found in brackish water in bays and tidal lagoons, as well as inland habitats.

Distribution
The buttonwood grows in tropical or subtropical regions around the world. It can be found along the Atlantic and Gulf Coasts of Florida and in Texas, as well the Bahamas, the Caribbean, the Atlantic and Pacific Coasts in South America, the Galapagos Islands, Polynesia, West Africa, and Kuwait.

FLOWERING DOGWOOD

Cornus florida

Avg height: 20–40 ft (6–12 m)
Avg trunk diameter: 9–12 in (23–30 cm)
Lifespan: 60–80 years

Bark: The bark of this tree is dark brown to dark gray in color. It has ridges on its surface and the plate of the bark is rectangular or square in shape. The bark has small scaly blocks as it matures.

Foliage: The leaves are oval in shape and bright green in color, turning a rich red-brown in the fall. They have smooth or wavy margins. The leaves can grow to be 2.4–5.1 in long (6–13 cm) and 1.6–2.4 in (4–6 cm) wide.

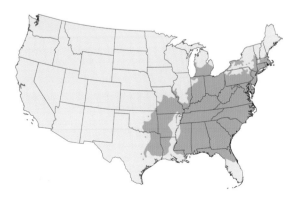

Flowers and fruit: The small fruit is green or red to burgundy in color. This shiny fruit is grown in clusters of 3 or 4 and is inedible for humans, but popular among birds and animals. The flowers of this tree come in a variety of colors, including yellow, green, pink, and white. They bloom in spring and have 4 long bracts. The buds of the flowers are round and flat.

Cornus florida, commonly known as the flowering dogwood, Virginia dogwood, Florida dogwood, or American boxwood, is an understory flowering tree that is small and deciduous. When mature, the flowering dogwood is usually broader than it is tall. The leaves of this tree face in opposing directions and are simple ovals in shape, with smooth or wavy margins. When found in the wild, the tree grows at the forest's edge. The flowering dogwood produces both flowers and fruit. Bracts of the tree are usually spread beyond the leaves. The Latin word *Cornus* references the tree's hard and dense wood.

INTERESTING FACTS

• The flowering dogwood, while classified as in the dogwood genus *Cornus*, is sometimes also classified in the *Benthamidia* genus.

• When propagating the flowering dogwood, its seeds are sown into rows of sawdust or sand.

• It was commonly used in medicine by the Native Americans.

HABITAT AND DISTRIBUTION

Habitat
The flowering dogwood grows ideally in moist, acidic, and well-drained soils with some amount of shade, but plenty of sunlight. Intense heat does not bode well for this tree. They often grow in the understory on middle and lower slopes, as well as in dry to wet woods, and while it grows best in moist soils, it will tolerate drier habitats.

Distribution
Native to eastern North America and northern Mexico, the flowering dogwood was once widely spread from the southern coast of Maine to Florida and west to the Mississippi River. It is widely grown in the temperate region of the continent. It can be found in Ontario Canada, the Mexican Gulf, and many states across the U.S. including New York, New Jersey, Ohio, Oklahoma, and Florida, Illinois, Kansas, North and South Carolina, Texas, and Kentucky.

COMMON PERSIMMON

Diospyros virginiana

Avg height: 30–80 ft (9–24 m)
Avg trunk diameter: 10–24 in (25–61 cm)
Lifespan: 60–75 years

Bark: The bark of the common persimmon is dark brown, black, or dark gray. Its plates are scaly on the surface. The branches can vary in color from reddish-brown to light brown or ashy gray depending on their maturity. The bark has vertical fissures and it is known for being sharp and bitter.

Foliage: The leaves of the common persimmon are oval-shaped. They can grow to be between 2.5–5 in (6.4–12.8 cm) in length and 0.75–2 in (1.9–5 cm) in width. The leaves grow in alternate directions. They are a vibrant, dark green above and pale or whitened below.

Fruit and flowers: The flowers of the common persimmon can range from white to greenish-white in color. They are shaped like blueberry flowers and grow on short stalks. The common persimmon is known for its fruit, which is a yellow to orange color. It is usually ripe in September or October and is edible. However, when eaten before ripening, it can be bitter and astringent.

Diospyros virginiana, otherwise known as common persimmon, is a small to medium-sized tree. Common persimmon has a short trunk that has widely spreading and crooked branches that create a round canopy when the tree reaches full maturity. The roots of this tree are heavy and stoloniferous (produces stolons or runners). Leaves on mature trees are thick and dark green, sometimes turning orange to bright red in fall, however they sometimes drop without changing color. The common persimmon is usually recognized by its bright yellow or orange fruit, which until it becomes over-ripe or suffers the effect of frost, is generally inedible due to its rather bitter taste.

INTERESTING FACTS

• The Greek word "Diospyros" means food of the gods, which is a nod to the orange fruit produced by the common persimmon.

• In traditional folklore, one can predict the weather using a seed of a persimmon. If the kernel is spoon-shaped, hard winter with heavy snowfall is predicted. If it is knife-shaped, expect a winter with frigid winds. If it is fork-shaped, mild winter with light, powdery snow is predicted.

• Persimmons are used to make a variety of dishes, including pies, puddings, cakes, cookies, salads, curries, and as a topping for breakfast cereal.

• The seeds were used as buttons during the American Civil War in the South.

HABITAT AND DISTRIBUTION

Habitat
While the common persimmon grows well in moist, well-drained, and sandy soils, it can survive in a dramatic range of conditions, including moist or very dry locations, rocky hillsides, dry or sandy woodlands, and river bottoms.

Distribution
Common persimmon is native to Florida and eastern Texas. It ranges from Florida to Connecticut and from Florida west to Texas through Iowa, Kansas, Oklahoma, and Louisiana.

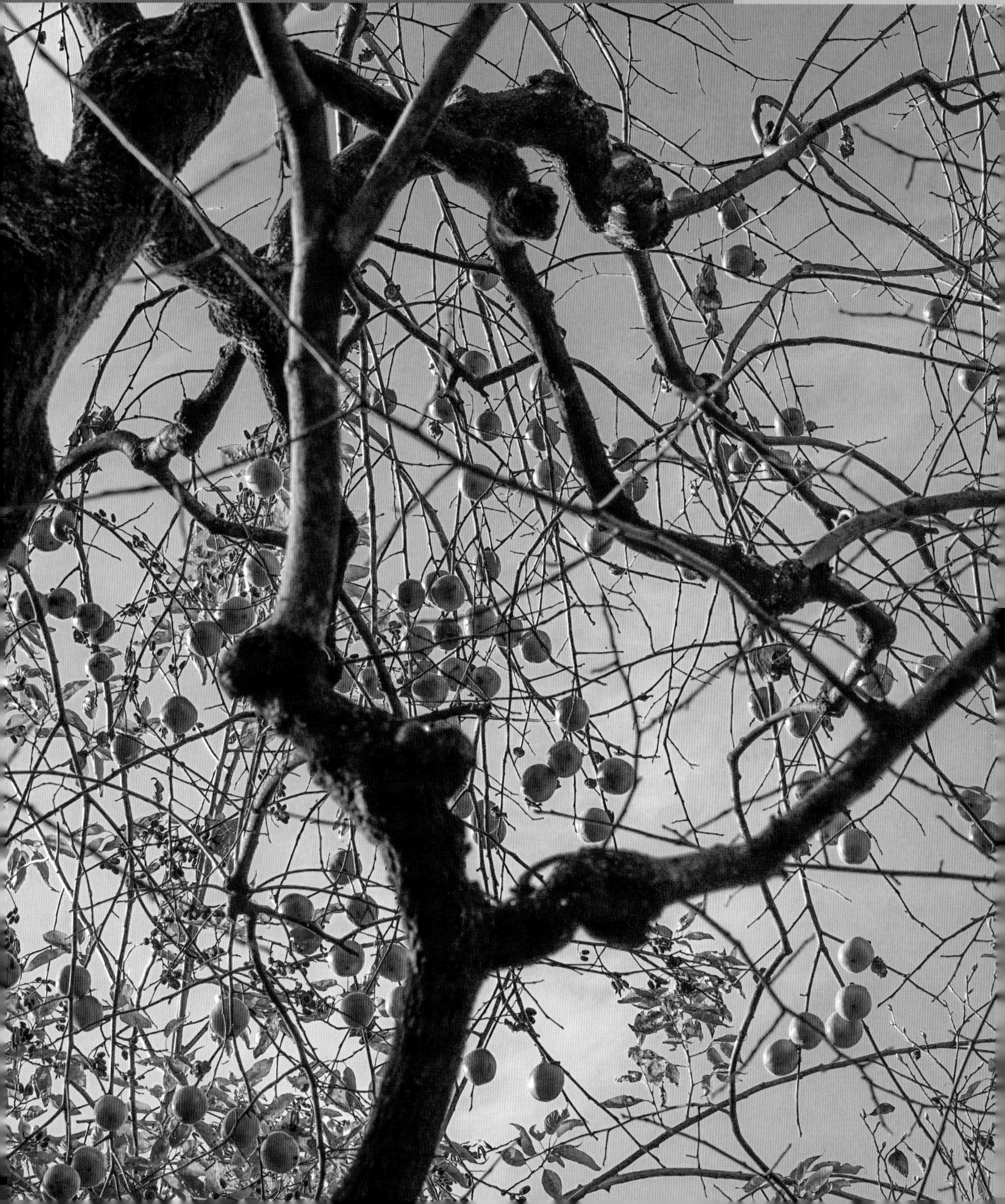

PACIFIC MADRONE
Arbutus menziesii

Avg height: 80–125 ft (24.4–38 m)
Avg trunk diameter: 24–48 in (61–122 cm)
Lifespan: 200–250 years

Bark: The Pacific madrone is well known for its flaky reddish-brown bark. When mature, the bark peels away to reveal a unique layer of smooth copper-colored bark underneath.

Foliage: The Pacific madrone has waxy evergreen foliage, dark green above and silvery-green below. The thick leaves are oval in shape and can grow to be 2.8–5.9 in (7–15 cm) long and 1.6–3.1 in (4–8 cm) wide.

Flowers and fruit: The Pacific madrone produces sweet-smelling flowers that densely bloom. Its flowers are small, white and shaped like tiny urns. The tree produces a bright red berry that is eaten by many animals. It ripens in the fall, going from a yellowish-green color to a red or reddish-orange.

Arbutus menziesii, commonly known as Pacific madrone or madrona, is an evergreen tree that is known for its striking beauty, particularly because of its signature reddish bark that peels away when mature to show the smoother copper–colored bark underneath. It is the largest flowering tree of the Ericaceae family. Its genus name *Arbutus* translates to strawberry, which references the bright red berries produced by the tree, with the color reminiscent of a strawberry. The berries develop hooked barbs when dry, which attach to animals and therefore aid dispersal. The Pacific madrone is one of the largest of the fourteen *Arbutus* species in the world; given the right conditions it can grow to 98 feet (30 meters).

INTERESTING FACTS

• Pacific madrone wood makes good firewood as it is a very dense and hard wood that burns slowly and hot. Large pieces of lumber tend to warp severely during the drying process so it is generally used only as veneer and flooring.

• The fruit is a favorite food source of many bird species in the Pacific Northwest, including band-tailed pigeons, doves, thrushes, robins, and quails. It is also used by cavity-nesting birds such as wrens, nuthatches, and woodpeckers.

• The leaves and bark of the tree have been used for medicinal purposes, including as a cold remedy and for stomach problems.

HABITAT AND DISTRIBUTION

Habitat
The Pacific madrone grows the best in warm, dry environments and it thrives in full sunlight. It prefers dry, sunny sites, and is often found on bluffs above the seashore, rocky coastal sites, wooded or exposed slopes, and canyons below 5,000 ft (1,524 m). It cannot tolerate flooding.

Distribution
Native to the west coast of North America from British Columbia to southern California through Washington and Oregon, the Pacific madrone is more commonly found at low elevations within 100 mi (161 km) of the Pacific coast.

Avg height: 12–20 ft (3.6–6.1 m)
Avg trunk diameter: 4–8 in (10–20 cm)
Lifespan: 60–75 years

MOUNTAIN LAUREL
Kalmia latifolia

The widely known flowering evergreen—*Kalmia latifolia* or mountain laurel—is commonly recognized as being an integral part of mountain landscape paintings. It grows to be a dense and rounded shrub and can grow to be a small-sized tree. Old mountain laurels may open to reveal a cracked and crooked trunk and branches. It usually has a compact and round crown. However, its distinguishing feature is its flowers. The showy and ornamental flowers are the reason for this shrub being a common addition to parks.

Bark: The bark of younger trees is dark reddis-brown. The thin, smooth bark of younger trees begins to shed as the tree ages. It also gets contorted as it grows and can often reveal a gnarly trunk and branches.

INTERESTING FACTS

• The mountain laurel is the state flower of Connecticut.

• The mountain laurel's flower has a unique way of distributing its pollen; the stamens fling pollen like a catapult when an insect sits on the flower's petal.

• This tree has a high flammability rating.

• All parts of the tree are highly toxic if ingested.

Foliage: The leaves can grow to be 1.2–4.7 in (3–12 cm) long and 5.5 in (14 cm) broad. The leaves remain a vibrant glossy green color all year round. They are leathery in texture and have an elliptic shape. They grow in alternate directions. They are vivid green above and yellowish-green below.

HABITAT AND DISTRIBUTION

Habitat
The mountain laurel is commonly found in open rocky or sandy woods, chilly meadows, mountain slopes, acidic forests and the borders of woodlands. It prefers soil that is acidic with a pH level ranging between 4.5 and 5.5. The tree is shade tolerant.

Flowers: The mountain laurel is most well known for its dense clusters of flowers. The fused-petal blossoms range from white to pink to rose red in color. The flowers often have maroon or purple spots and lines. The fruit from this tree is small, brown, or copper in color and shaped like a capsule.

Distribution
The mountain laurel is native to eastern North America and can be found from southern Maine south to northern Florida, and west from southern Indiana south to eastern Louisiana. It is naturally found on the rocky slopes and forests of mountains.

Avg height: 25–30 ft (7.6–9.1 m)
Avg trunk diameter: 15–20 in (38–51 cm)
Lifespan: 100–200 years

SOURWOOD
Oxydendrum arboreum

The sourwood or sorrel tree is the only species in the genus *Oxydendrum* and a member of the Ericaceae family. Oxydendrum is derived from the Greek words *Oxys* and *Dendron*, which mean acid and tree respectively, while the species name comes from the Latin word arboreus, meaning of a tree. The sourwood is a deciduous small tree has leaves that have a sour taste (thus the name sourwood). The tree has something to offer in all seasons, with esthetic flowers that bloom in the summer, color changing leaves in the fall and fruit capsules in the winter. The flowers of the sourwood contribute to its beauty. What makes the sourwood unique is the fact that the leaves lean down from the branches, giving the tree a weeping willow look.

Bark: Sourwood bark is gray with a hint of red. It has deep lines and is scaly. The branches can be light yellow or green at the start, but mature into a reddish-brown color.

INTERESTING FACTS

• The juice taken from the blooms of the sourwood is used to make sourwood jelly, and the tree is renowned for its nectar and the honey which is produced from it.

• Pioneers found many uses for the different parts of this tree, including using the sap to treat fevers, bark for mouth pain, and tea from the leaves for stomach diseases.

• In the Appalachian region, the sourwood is referenced in a popular old-time tune called the Sourwood Mountain, a traditional American folk song that is a lament over the singer's true love from whom he is separated.

Foliage: The leaves are vibrant green and turn yellow, red and purple in the fall. Oblong or elliptical leaves are arranged alternately and can grow to an average size of 3.1–7.9 in (8–20 cm) long and 1.6–3.5 in (4–9 cm) wide. The margins are thinly serrated.

HABITAT AND DISTRIBUTION

Habitat
This deciduous tree grows the best when there is little to no root competition. It prefers peat soils with high acidic content, normal moisture retention, and good drainage. It has moderate drought tolerance. Full sunlight exposure is ideal, with at least six hours of direct exposure per day.

Fruit: Sourwood grows white, pleasant-smelling flowers on drooping stalks in the early summer. The fruit this tree yields is small, woody, and capsule shaped.

Distribution
Sourwood is native to the eastern U.S. and can be commonly found on the lower chain of the Appalachian Mountains. It can be found in southern Pennsylvania to northern Florida, west to southern Illinois, from West Virginia and Kentucky south to eastern Louisiana and the Gulf coasts of Mississippi and Alabama.

AMERICAN CHESTNUT
Castanea dentata

Avg height: 50–80 ft (15.25–24.4 m)
Avg trunk diameter: 16–40 in (40.6–101.6 cm) **Lifespan:** 250–500 years

A tall deciduous tree belonging to the Fagaceae family, *Castanea dentata* or American chestnut was once known as the finest chestnut tree in the world and is ideal for forests. Before 1900, the American chestnut was one of the most essential forest trees in North America. However, a deadly fungal disease that targeted the bark of the tree spread from the Japanese and Chinese chestnut trees, and was first discovered in New York in 1904. Within 40 years, between 3 and 4 billion American chestnut trees were wiped out. Some trees, however, were found in Michigan, where the fungus was found to be less virulent because it was being controlled by a virus.

Bark: The bark is light gray and has flat ridges around the trunk. It is smooth when the tree is younger but becomes rough and furrowed as the tree matures.

Foliage: The oblong leaves can grow to 5.5–8 in (14–20 cm) long and 3–4 in (7–10 cm) wide. The leaves are alternate, with serrated margins and bristled tips.

HABITAT AND DISTRIBUTION

Habitat
The ideal habitat for the American chestnut included loamy, acidic, and well-drained soil. Full sun exposure is required, with at least 6 hours of exposure and 2–6 hours of partial shade. The American chestnut is commonly found in coastal, mountainous, and piedmont regions.

Flowers: The tree also produces pleasant-smelling yellowish-white male flowers in slender catkin clusters. small, woody, and capsule-shaped.

Fruit: The fruit of this tree is the American chestnut. It is brown or copper in color and edible and sweet in taste, encased in spiny burrs.

Distribution
The American chestnut was once one of the most common trees in the northeastern states of the U.S. Very few chestnuts now grow in its historical range from Massachusetts and Pennsylvania south to Alabama and Mississippi, but there are hundreds outside its former range, such as in northern Michigan.

Avg height: 60–80 ft (18.3–24.4 m)
Avg trunk diameter: 24–36 in (61–91.4 cm)
Lifespan: 400–500 years

Bark: The giant chinkapin has thin bark that has a smoother texture on younger trees. As the tree matures, the bark becomes thicker and plates begin to appear that are reddish in color. It has been found to be one of the most significant factors contributing to the survival of the species.

Foliage: The leathery leaves are dark green in color on the surface, but golden and fuzzy underneath. They are folded upward from the middle. They have a lanceolate to oblong shape and the leaves can grow to be 2–6 in (5–15 cm) long.

Flowers and fruit: The giant chinkapin yields white male flowers that grow in upright catkins with clusters of female flowers growing under the male flowers. One to three nuts are produces in the fall, encased in a spiny burr resembling that of chestnuts.

GIANT CHINKAPIN
Castanopsis chrysophylla

A member of the Fagaceae family, the *Castanopsis chrysophylla* or giant chinkapin is the only species in its genus that is the size of a tree. The giant chinkapin is an evergreen tree that has distinctive leaves. *Castanopsis* means resembling chestnuts, while its latin name is derived from chysolepis, which means golden scales. *Chrysophylla* means golden leaves, referring to the golden underside of the chinkapin's leaves. The crown of the tree is cone shaped and open, giving it a distinct shape and asserting dominance, even in conditions with little competition. The giant chinkapin can be found as a tree or a shrub.

INTERESTING FACTS

• The nut of the giant chinkapin tastes similar to hazelnuts and is often enjoyed by squirrels, chipmunks and other small mammal denizens of California and southern Oregon.

• While the wood from the giant chinkapin is sturdy and hard, it is rarely found in large enough quantities to be used for commercial purposes.

HABITAT AND DISTRIBUTION

Habitat
The giant chinkapin is adaptable to harsh, drought-prone, or infertile habitats. It can grow in a range of soils, but ideally prefers deep soils. It can usually be found in climax forests, coastal forests, woodlands, and chaparral. It is best grown in habitats of mixed tree species..

Distribution
The giant chinkapin is native to the Pacific coast of the U.S. and grows from southern Washington to western Oregon. It can also be found in south to west-central California. The tree is commonly found in the western Cascade ranges.

AMERICAN BEECH
Fagus grandifolia

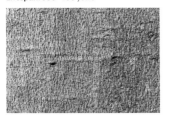

Avg height: 52–115 ft (16–35 m)
Avg trunk diameter: 20–48 in (50–120 cm)
Lifespan: 300–400 years

Bark: The American beech is known for its smooth and pale silver bark, which manages to retain these qualities even into old age. The thin bark makes it vulnerable to fire.

Foliage: The leaves are dark-green and glossy, with a distinct oblong shape, veiny surface, and sawlike edges. They are usually darker on top and lighter green on the bottom. The branches grow horizontally.

Flowers and fruit: Flowers appear in the very early spring, at the same time as new leaves begin to unfold. The male flowers are small and yellow; the even smaller female flowers are reddish. Beech nuts are eaten by squirrels, bears, and other mammals.

Buds: Beech buds are distinctly thin and long, resembling cigars; this characteristic makes beech trees relatively easy to identify.

Fagus grandifolia or American beech is a sturdy and impressive tree, native to eastern North America, that can easily grow to 90 ft (27 m) tall. Its wide canopy provides a cool shade during the summer, while its distinctively oblong leaves turn from their characteristic dark green color into beautiful shades of yellow and orange in the fall. Due to their attractive foliage, they are planted in parks and golf courses across the country. Something to look for when attempting to determine whether a tree is an American beech is the shape of the buds: beech buds are particularly thin and long, like very slim cigars. The beech tree grows in a naturally oval shape and requires plenty of space to extend its branches.

INTERESTING FACTS

• Despite preferring light, the American beech is almost unrivaled when it comes to its shade tolerance.

• Due to the very slow growth rate of the tree—sometimes less than 12 in (30 cm) in a year—it is not considered a good choice for a quick transformation of a green landscape. Rather, it is a tree many choose to plant as a legacy to future generations. However, what it lacks in growth speed, it more than compensates in longevity.

• Unlike most trees, beeches retain their smooth bark even in old age. Many hold it close to their heart for this reason, as it is often a favorite choice among those looking to carve initials and dates on a tree.

HABITAT AND DISTRIBUTION

Habitat
Fagus grandifolia tends to prefer a rich loamy soil. Despite being extremely tolerant of shade, it tends to grow best in full sun to medium shade. The American beech tends to prefer moist, well-drained environments, and doesn't do well in wet or compacted soil. It can be found in shady riverbanks, moist mountain coves, the areas in swamps with better drainage, and rich mesic woodlands. It usually grows in unmixed stands or association with sugar maples and other hardwoods.

Distribution
Native to eastern North America, the American beech can be found from Nova Scotia west to Maine, Southern Ontario in Canada, west to Wisconsin and south to eastern Texas and northern Florida. There is also a variety of beech tree that grows in the mountains of northeastern Mexico, called *Fagus mexicana*.

Avg height: 49–82 ft (15–25 m)
Avg trunk diameter: 24–75 in (60–190 cm)
Lifespan: 250–350 years

Bark: The mature bark is a brown/gray color, and is moderately thick with narrow furrows growing in thin plates with flattened to rounded ridges that are slightly lighter than the rest of the bark.

Foliage: Tanoaks are evergreen trees, with leaves that persist through the winter. The leaves have toothed edges and a hard texture that is often compared to leather. The dull green leaves are covered in brown or orange, dense scruffy hairs that eventually wear off in the top part of the leaf.

Flowers and fruit: Male and female flowers are borne on the same tree. Male flowers release pollen, carried by wind to female flowers. The fruit is an acorn 0.75–1.18 in (2–3 cm) long and 0.75 in (2 cm) in diameter, with a very hard woody shell. It sits in a rough, spiny cup until maturation 18 months later, when it falls to the ground and may be dispersed by birds or rodents.

TANOAK
Notholithocarpus densiflorus

Notholithocarpus densiflorus, commonly known as the tanoak tree, is an evergreen hardwood tree that is often regarded as an evolutionary link between oaks and chestnuts. A West Coast native, it produces an acorn seed that can look like an oak acorn but has a harder, thick shell that most resembles a hazelnut. Often mistaken for an oak, the tree was a major source of income for mountain people due to the leather tanning qualities of its bark. This, however, came at an environmental cost: most trees were cut down to turn hides into leather. By the early 20th century, the excessive use of the tree began to subside due to the scarcity of mature tanoak trees and the development of synthetic tannins.

INTERESTING FACTS

• Historically, people preferred the tanoak acorns over others. The Hupa Native American people used the tanoak acorns in baking, to make bread, biscuits, and cakes.

• The acorns are bitter and inedible when not leached but are often eaten by squirrels. Roasted, they can be eaten as is or used as a coffee substitute.

• The tanoak is one of the species most vulnerable to "sudden oak death" disease. The origin of the disease is still unclear, although it is believed it was introduced by foreign species.

HABITAT AND DISTRIBUTION

Habitat
Notholithocarpus densiflorus prefers moist mixed evergreen forests and is typically associated with hazelnut trees, Pacific rhododendron, manzanita, and huckleberry. This species grows best in Mediterranean climates modified by cool and moist coastal air currents. It favors moist and humid soils, and environments with rain, fog, and/or high humidity. Unlike true oaks, it requires very deep soils to dig its roots.

Distribution
The tanoak tree is a native species in the western U.S., from southwest Oregon to the California Coast Range. It can be found as far south as the Transverse Ranges in California, north to southwest Oregon, and east to the Sierra Nevada. Inland populations grow through the Siskiyou Mountains. They can grow from sea level up to an elevation of 8,000 ft (2,438 m).

SOUTHERN LIVE OAK

Quercus virginiana

Avg height: 40–80 ft (12–24 m)
Avg trunk diameter: 48–78 in (122–200 cm) **Lifespan:** 300–500 years

Bark: In young trees, the bark has red-brown furrows with small surface scales. With age, the bark becomes dark gray or black and thick, with blocky scales and deep furrows.

Foliage: Leaves remain through winter but drop and are replaced over a short period of several weeks in the spring. The leaves reach 2–5 in (5–10 cm) in length and are elliptical or oblong, coming to a tapered point.

Flowers and fruit: Female flowers are small and yellowish-green, and bloom in spring. Male flowers hang in catkins 2.75–5 in (7–10 cm) long.. Pollen is dispersed by wind, usually in early spring. Acorns produced annually in September, fall in December, and are eaten by animals. They are 0.75 in (1.9 cm) long and have a warty cap.

Quercus virginiana, commonly known as the southern live oak, Virginia live oak, plateau oak, scrub live oak, escarpment live oak, that is native to the southeastern U.S. and northern Mexico is considered a symbolic tree of the southern U.S. It is the best known of the "live oaks," a loose term used for any oak species that is evergreen in at least part of its range. Trunks are short and often gnarled with rough and cracked bark and frequently showing roots in the form of buttresses. The trunk supports branches that spread horizontally with not only its own dense foliage but also clumps of ball moss and drapings of Spanish moss, forming a rounded and wide crown. The wood is hard and difficult to saw so it is little used commercially and is mainly used to produce charcoal.

INTERESTING FACTS

• The largest living southern live oak is the Seven Sisters Oak, found in Mandeville, Louisiana. It stands at 57 ft (17.4 m) with a diameter of 12.6 ft (3.8 m) and a spread exceeding 153 ft (46.6 m). The Seven Sisters was estimated to be between 500 and 1,000 years old.

- Located in Rockport, Texas, stands the "Big Tree," one of the most famous live oaks in the world. Named "Texas State Champion Virginia Live Oak" in 1969, it is both one of the largest living oak trees and the oldest, with recent estimates placing it between 1,000 to 2,000 years old.

HABITAT AND DISTRIBUTION

Habitat
It grows in acid, neutral or alkaline soils, though it grows best in soils with high content of organic matter. It can be found on flat areas and steep slopes alike. It is tolerant of salt so it can dominate in coastal forest climates although it is intolerant of sea winds. It best grows in deep soils, although it can also be found in shallow soils. The live oak grows in both mixed and single species forests in a range of soils from heavy textures to sands.

Distribution
The southern live oak can be found in the lower East Coast of the U.S. and the Gulf of Mexico, particularly along the lower coastal plains. Its native range extends from Virginia in a narrow band south through North Carolina along the coast. From the interior South Carolina coast, its range extends further inland as it moves south, crossing southern Georgia, all of Florida, southern Mississippi, southern Louisiana, and part of Texas.

Avg height: 60–90 ft (18–27 m)
Avg trunk diameter: 24–36 in (61–91 cm)
Lifespan: 200–400 years

Bark: The bark ranges from dark gray to brownish-gray to dark reddish-brown in color. On young trees and large stems, the bark is light gray and smooth. Rounded, scaly ridges separated by shallow fissures develop as the tree ages. As the tree becomes fully mature, the bark turns to a dark brown in color.

Foliage: The leaves are alternately arranged and ovate to elliptical. Each leaf has 7–9 shallow lobes, tipped with bristles. The leaves are 5–10 in (12.5–25 cm) long and 5–7 in (12.5–18 cm) wide. They are dark green above and paler green below, with both sides smooth with minute hairs, particularly on the veins below. In fall, leaves turn russet red, bright red, or brown.

NORTHERN RED OAK
Quercus rubra

Quercus rubra, or northern red oak, is the second most common species of oak in the northeastern U.S., following the pin oak (*Quercus palustris*). It is a highly branched tree, large or medium in size, with a wide oval or rounded crown in wide growing conditions; the crown is narrower and taller if the tree grows in dense forests. This oak grows straight and tall, with open-grown trees having a stouter trunk and slightly less height. Stout branches grow at right angles to the trunk. It is a rapidly growing tree and may grow as much as 24 in (61 cm) a year for 10 years. It is valued for its hardiness and adaptability in urban settings and is one of the most important oaks for timber production, used for veneer, flooring, and furniture. It is valuable to wildlife and is the state tree of New Jersey.

INTERESTING FACTS

• In spite of their impressive size, northern red oaks can thrive in cities given enough space, as they are tolerant of compacted soils and pollution.

• The Native American Potawatomi tribe used the bark of the tree to treat sore throat, flux, and sores. The bark was used externally to wash the skin for burns or eruptions, or chewed to heal mouth sores.

• The acorns are good food sources for a wide variety of wildlife, including raccoons, ruffed grouse, fox squirrels, blue jays, bears, and wild turkeys, while deer consume the twigs during winter.

HABITAT AND DISTRIBUTION

Habitat
The northern red oak grows fastest and tallest in a totally sunny location. Although it can tolerate many soils, it does best along well-drained stream banks. It is grown in public or private gardens, as an isolated specimen, or in groups in large and wide spaces. It is a very decorative and ornamental tree, especially in fall because of the magnificent coloring of its leaves that creates an extraordinary focal point.

Distribution
The range of the northern red oak extends from the northeastern U.S., west to the Great Lakes and Minnesota, as far north as southeastern Canada to Nova Scotia, and south to Arkansas, Alabama, and Georgia.

Flowers and fruit: Male flowers appear in spring before leaves in yellowish, drooping catkins. Female flowers develop in clusters of one to three as small, red buds lacking petals. Acorns begin light green and mature to brown 18 months after pollination, occurring singly or in pairs. The reddish-brown acorn caps are saucer shaped and cover less than a quarter of the acorn.

Avg height: 50—100 ft (15.25—30.5 m)
Avg trunk diameter: 39—78 in (100—200 cm)
Lifespan: 300—500 years

Bark: Bark is whitish or ashy gray. On larger stems it is irregularly plated, and on smaller stems it is scaly. While the bark is generally scaly with platelets of bark that can peel away from the trunk, smooth patches are not uncommon even on older trees.

Foliage: Leaves are green above and whitish below. They are oblong to ovate in shape and are alternately arranged on the branch. Each leaf has 7—10 rounded lobes with the depth between ranging from deep to shallow. The base of the leaf is wedge-shaped and the apex is generally rounded. Each leaf reaches 4—7 in (10—17.75 cm) in length.

Flowers and fruit: Flowers appear in spring and depend on the wind for pollination. Female flowers are reddish-green, appearing as small single spikes, and develop with the leaves in mid-spring. Yellow-green male flowers grow in catkins 2—4 in (5—10 cm) long. The acorns grow at the end of certain peduncles and mature after around 6 months. Their warty cap covers a quarter of the acorn and detaches at maturity.

WHITE OAK
Quercus alba

Quercus alba, commonly known as American white oak or simply white oak, is a species of oak in the Fagaceae family. Although it is called white oak, it is unusual to find one with completely white bark, because the color is typically pale gray. Typical of all oaks in the *Quercus* (white oak) subgenus, they have comparatively long acorns with short styles that ripen in a single growing season, and the lobes of its leaves are rounded, not pointed, It is considered the most valuable and majestic oak in North America. In dense forests, the white oak can grow to a huge height and in an open setting it can grow particularly wide with very leafy branches. While its height alone is impressive, it can spread out to enormous widths as its branches grow parallel to the ground. Together, these branches form a rugged, irregular crown.

HABITAT AND DISTRIBUTION

Habitat
The white oak grows in a diversity of terrains, preferring low, dry, or moist soils. It has been found in altitudes up to 5,250 ft (1,600 m) in the Appalachian Mountains. White oak grows best in soils that are neutral or only moderately acidic or alkaline. It prefers north and east-facing lower coves and slopes and is able to grow on all upland aspects and slope positions within its range.

Distribution
The white oak is found over most of the eastern U.S. It can be found from southwestern Maine to extreme southern Quebec, west to southern Ontario, Michigan, and southeastern Minnesota; south to western Iowa, Missouri, Oklahoma, and Texas; and east to northern Florida and Georgia.

PIN OAK
Quercus palustris

Avg height: 59–72 ft (18–22 m)
Avg trunk diameter: up to 39 in (1 m)
Lifespan: up to 120 years

Bark: Pin oak bark is smooth when young but becomes rougher by the time it is 40 years old.

Leaves: Each leaf has five or seven lobes, each with 5–7 bristle–tipped teeth, and rounded and very deep-cut sinuses between the lobes. Mostly hairless; turn bronze in fall.

Catkins: Male flowers are borne in catkins that appear at the same time in spring as the leaves; female flowers are wind-pollinated.

Acorns: Hemispherical acorns are 0.4–0.6 in (10–16 mm) wide in a shallow, thin cap and mature from green to dark brown 18 months after pollination.

Quercus palustris, also known as pin oak or swamp Spanish oak. It is in the red oak group, which all have acorns that mature in 18 months and bristle-tipped lobes. However, it can be distinguished from the others by its leaves, which are perhaps the extreme of the lobed shape associated with the oak tree in that the sinuses—the spaces between the lobes—are so deeply cut that they reach nearly back to the main vein, so that the sinus, or empty, area is as big as the leaf area. The acorns of pin oaks are eaten by birds such as jays and turkeys and mammals including squirrels and mice. In addition, various birds, from warblers to the Swainson's Hawk in size, nest in the pin oak, as do wetland birds such as herons and egrets that nest in colonies in trees.

INTERESTING FACTS

• The bark was used by some Native American tribes to make a drink to treat intestinal pain.

• The wood is hard and heavy, so it is used for both general building and firewood.

• The wood was used to make pins used in construction, possibly leading to the name "pin oak."

• The pin oak is eaten by many different insects—including the caterpillars of the Bucculatri domicola moth, for which it is the only known food plant.

HABITAT AND DISTRIBUTION

Habitat
Pin oaks grow primarily on level, poorly drained soils with high clay content, which, as a result, are particularly wet in winter and spring. They are most common on sites that are flooded periodically during the dormant season but not during the growing season, a habitat which is known as "pin oak flats" for that reason.

Distribution
The pin oak is primarily in the eastern and central U.S., from Connecticut south to North Carolina and Tennessee, and west to Missouri, eastern Kansas, and eastern Oklahoma.

OAK LEAVES AND ACORNS

The oak (*Quercus*) genus is represented by approximately 500 trees and shrubs worldwide, including 70 trees that are native to North America, All oaks have pinnate leaves—one long vein goes the full length of the leaf from the stem to the leaf tip—and most are lobed. The large number of species are grouped into six subgenera, sorted depending on the structure of the acorns and how long they take to ripen; the oaks in North America are in two of these six: the subgenera *Quercus* and *Lobatae*, commonly called white and red oaks.

The acorns of white oaks ripen in the fall after a single growing season, the inside of the cap is smooth, and the style is short. Red oaks have acorns that ripen in the fall after the second growing season, the inside of the cap is hairy, and the style is long. Some oaks are evergreen rather than deciduous, and are called "live oaks"; however, this is not a separate subgenus—some live oaks are white oaks, and others are red oaks.

WHITE OAKS (*subgenus Quercus***)**
Despite the wide variety in acorn shape, the inside of the cap of all white oak acorns is smooth and they have a short style. These acorns ripen in the fall after only a single growing season. Most are deciduous, but the Southern Live Oak (*Quercus virginiana*) is evergreen (as are all so-called "live" oaks) and has narrow pinnate leaves.

White Oak *Quercus alba*

Swamp White Oak *Quercus bicolor*

Overcup Oak *Quercus lyrata*

Bur Oak *Quercus macrocarpa*

Common Chinkapin Oak *Quercus muehlenbergii*

Common Post Oak *Quercus stellata*

Southern Live Oak *Quercus virginiana*

RED OAKS *(subgenus Lobatae)*
Regardless of their shape, all acorns of the subgenus Lobatae have a cap that is hairy on the inside and a long style. Acorns in the red oak group ripen in the fall after the second growing season. One of the most common evergreen oaks in the red oak group is the Coast Live Oak, notable for its especially long pointed acorns..

Northern Red Oak *Quercus rubra*

Scarlet Oak *Quercus coccinea*

Pin Oak *Quercus palustris*

Laurel Oak *Quercus laurifolia*

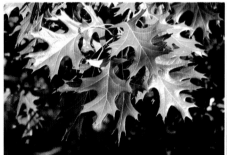

Black Oak *Quercus velutina*

Water Oak *Quercus nigra*

Coast Live Oak *Quercus agrifolia*

WITCH-HAZEL

Hamamelis virginiana

Avg height: 10—25 ft (3—7.5 m)
Avg trunk diameter: 6—8 in (15—20 cm)
Lifespan: 400—500 years

Bark: The bark is smooth and scaly, light brown to light gray in color. The inner bark is reddish-purple. The bark is used for a variety of purposes.

Foliage: Its leaves are oval, oblique at the base and either pointed or rounded at the tip, ranging widely in size. They are 1.5—6.5 in (3.8—16.5 cm) long and 1—5 in (2.5—13 cm) broad, with shallowly toothed edges. The leaves are alternate with short petioles falling off before flowering.

Flowers and Fruit: The witch hazel produces pale to bright yellow flowers between 0.5—0.75 in (1—2 cm) in length, with 4 petals. The flowers appear in late fall when the leaves have detached, and show narrow, elongated yellow petals and orange sepals which produce woody fruit, in the shape of a pointed capsule that opens at the half. When the fruit matures, one year after polliation, it explodes from pressure from its walls and expels its 2 black seeds at a long distance up to 33 ft (10 m).

Hamamelis virginiana, commonly known as witch-hazel, winterbloom, or snapping hazelnut, is a small deciduous tree or shrub of the Hamamelidaceae family. The witch hazel is a plant that became fashionable in the nineteenth century. Its delicate yellow blossoms open in the fall, just as the leaves of other deciduous trees are changing color and dropping; its blossoms persist after its own leaves drop as well. It is often multi-trunked and has large, crooked, spreading branches that reach 15—20 ft (4.5—6 m) and form an irregular, open crown. There are 62 different species of caterpillars that eat witch-hazel leaves, deer and beavers also browse on the leaves, while birds and small mammals eat the fruits and and seeds.

INTERESTING FACTS

• Native Americans used this plant to make a medicinal tea, used to treat burns, boils, and wounds of all kinds. Early settlers to New England adopted this practice.

• It is possible that the common name witch-hazel was given because its branches were once used as divining rods for the detection of underground water.

• An astringent liniment, witch-hazel is an alcohol extract of the bark and is commercially used in aftershave lotions, eye-washes, medicines, and in salves for soothing poison ivy rashes, burns, and insect bites.

HABITAT AND DISTRIBUTION

Habitat
Witch-hazel grows most commonly on riverbanks and forest edges. The tree grows best in full sun to partial shade and wet, somewhat acidic soil. It also thrives in temperate zones in damp or marshy woods.

Distribution
Hamamelis virginiana is found throughout eastern North America, from Nova Scotia in Canada, west to Wisconsin, and south to Louisiana, Alabama, and Florida. *H. virginiana var. mexicana* is native to Texas and northern Mexico..

Avg height: 60—75 ft (18—22 m)
Avg trunk diameter: 18—36 in (45—91 cm)
Lifespan: 200—300 years

Bark: The bark is light brown tinted with red or gray with black streaks with scaly ridges and is extensively fissured. The bark adheres to the tree's short branches and twigs in vertical plates and a section of the leafless branch can look like a reptile's scales, causing the tree to be referred to as "alligator wood."

Foliage: The leaves feature five strongly pointed palmate lobes on average, with three or seven on rare occasion. The leaves are 3—5 in (8–13 cm) wide. In the fall, the glossy, star-shaped leaves change from dark green to yellow, orange, red, or purple.

Flowers and fruit: The flowers bloom in the spring and last throughout the fall and occasionally into the winter. They usually have a diameter of 1–1.6 in (2.5–4 cm) and are coated with rusty hairs. The blooms are greenish in color and unisexual. The unusual complex fruit is hard, dry, and globose, with a diameter of 1–1.6 in (2.5–4 cm) and with between 40–60 capsules. Each capsule contains one or two tiny seeds.

SWEET GUM
Liquidambar styraciflua

Liquidambar styraciflua, commonly called American sweetgum, is a deciduous tree native to Mexico's tropical highlands south to Central America. Hazel pine, American storax, bilsted, redgum, satin-walnut, star-leaved gum, and alligator wood are some of its other names. Sweetgum is a popular ornamental tree in temperate climates and one of the most valuable forest plants in the Southeast. Its five-pointed star-shaped leaves (which resemble maple leaves) and robust, spiky fruits make it distinctive. It was formerly classified as a Hamamelidaceae member, but it is now classed as an Altingiaceae member. When the tree is damaged, the brownish-yellow gum resin for which the tree is named—both *Liquidambar* and sweet gum—seeps from the tree's bark.

INTERESTING FACTS

• The resin is type of natural balsam that looks like turpentine and is often called liquidamber.

• The sap is released when incisions in the bark are made.

• Native Americans used American sweetgum sap as chewing gum and utilized it to cure a variety of ailments.

• In the past, the bark and root of American sweetgum were used to cure diarrhea, fever, and skin problems.

HABITAT AND DISTRIBUTION

Habitat
It's widely grown in its native North America, as well as many other temperate regions across the world. The plant prefers wet, acidic loam or clay soil and can withstand poor drainage. Other coastal plain species like willow oak and sweetbay magnolia thrive beside it.

Distribution Sweetgum is one of the most common hardwoods in the Southeast, where it grows naturally in lowlands from southwestern Connecticut to central Florida, through southern Ohio and west to Illinois, southeastern Missouri, Arkansas, to eastern Texas, but not in the cooler Appalachian highlands or the Midwestern states. The species may also be found through eastern Mexico south to Central America.

Avg height: 40–60 ft (12–18 m)
Avg trunk diameter: 30 ft (12 m)
Lifespan: 80–100 yrs

Bark: The gray bark has seams that appear to separate the bark into flakes.

Foliage and fruit: The palmately compound leaves have five leaflets and are 3–6.3 in (8–16 cm) long and broad. Up to 3 nutlike seeds, brown with a white basal scar, are contained in a light green spiky shell of 1.6–2 in (4–5 cm) in diameter that turns a tan color in late summer and splits open.

Flowers: The Ohio buckeye is polygamo-monoecious: it has both bisexual flowers and ones that are only male. The flowers are borne on upright branched clusters of 4–8 in (10–20 cm) and only those near the base are perfect; the higher blossoms are only male.

OHIO BUCKEYE
Aesculus glabra

Aesculus glabra is also known as Ohio buckeye, American buckeye, and stinking buck-eye. It is a member of the Sapindaceae, or soapberry, family, which is spread around the world with 138 genera and more than 1,900 species. It may owe its derogatory common name to the noxious odor of the leaves when they are crushed. Other gardeners may try to eradicate it because of its toxicity to cattle and other livestock, or because the high density of fruit on the tree make it undesirable as a street tree. However, it is the state tree for Ohio and "buckeye" has been a part of the state lexicon since the first pioneers explored the frontier. The shell doesn't split open until it hits the ground. Squirrels are the only animals that are able to digest buckeyes and not be poisoned.

INTERESTING FACTS

• Although the seeds are poisonous because they contain tannic acid (as do the young foliage, shoots, and bark), the Lenape made an infusion of ground nuts mixed with sweet oil to treat earaches.

• The ground nuts were also used to poison fish, and they were blanched extract the tannic acid for use in making leather.

• The Lenape also made a kind of supplement to treat arthritis by cooking buckeyes, then beating them into a paste.

HABITAT AND DISTRIBUTION

Habitat
It needs well-drained, moist soil; it is often found growing near streams and rivers. It often grows as an understory tree, needing protection from full sun, and may be found along the edges of old fields.

Distribution
It is native to the Midwest and lower Great Plains, south to a band of dark, fertile soil that extends to the northern border of Alabama.

Avg height: 70–80 ft (21–24 m)
Avg trunk diameter: 2–3 ft (61–91 cm)
Lifespan: Up to 200 yrs

Bark: The shaggy and loose-plated bark for which the shagbark hickory is named is on mature trees; young trees have smooth bark.

Foliage and fruit: The unique palmate compound leaves are 12–24 in (30–60 cm) and have five finely toothed, lance-shaped, pointed pinnate leaflets; the terminal three much bigger than the basal two. The fruit is an edible nut, a drupe 1–1.5 in (2.5–4 cm) long with hard bony shell contained in thick green 4-sectioned husk that turns dark and splits off at maturity in the fall.

Flowers: monoecious, male flowers on long catkins on old wood or previous season's leaf axils and female flowers in short terminal spikes.

SHAGBARK HICKORY
Carya ovata

Carya ovata is also known as shagbark hickory, scalybark hickory, shellbark hickory, and Carolina hickory. While the first part of its common name obviously refers to the nature of the bark, "hickory" is shortened from pokahickory, which was an adaptation of the Algonquian word pawcohiccora, the hickory-nut meat. The hickory nut was a significant food source for the Algonquians, who also cooked with the kernel milk, and used it to smoke meat, and make their bows. The lumber is so heavy and hard that it has been used for tools that had to be resilient, such as plows, axles, and axe handles. Carolina shagbark hickory (*Carya ovata* var. *australis*), which is smaller overall than northern shagbark hickory (*C. ovata* var. *ovata*), is sometimes considered a separate species.

INTERESTING FACTS

• The shagbark hickory can grow well over 100 ft (30 m) tall—the tallest, in Savage Gulf, Tennessee, is more than 150 ft (46 m) tall.

• Although the usual lifespan is up to 200 years, the oldest tree found is 370 years old, in Fiddler's Green, Virginia.

• Many animals and birds eat the nuts, digesting them and thereby spreading the seeds: squirrels, raccoons, chipmunks, mice, black bears, foxes, rabbits, and birds such as ducks, bobwhites, and turkeys.

HABITAT AND DISTRIBUTION

Habitat
Shagbark hickories can tolerate partial shade and a range of temperatures but do best in humid temperatures with moist soils. However, they can tolerate average annual rainfalls ranging from 30 to 80 in (760–2,030 mm) and 20–40 in (510–1,020 mm) during the growing season.

Distribution
Shagbark hickory is found throughout most of the eastern and midwestern parts of the U.S., although neither the southeast or Gulf coastal plains nor the lower Mississippi Delta areas

Avg height: 50–66 ft (15–20 m)
Avg trunk diameter: 16–31 in (40–80 cm)
Lifespan: 50–75 years

Bark: Light gray or gray-brown with flat-topped, shiny ridges, which develop a diamond-shape pattern with age.

Leaves: Leaves are alternate and pinnately compound, 15–25 in (38–64 cm) long with 11–17 oblong-lanceolate leaflets, each serrated and broader than 0.4 in (1 cm).

Flowers: Male flowers grow in slender, yellow-green catkins. Female flowers are short terminal spikes growing from new shoots, each with a light pink stigma.

Fruit: In clusters of 2–6; oblong-ovoid nut is 1.25–2.25 in (3–6 cm) long and 0.75–1.5 in (2–4 cm) wide. The nut is encased by a green husk until it matures in mid-fall.

BUTTERNUT
Juglans cinerea

Juglans cinerea, commonly known as butternut or white walnut, is endemic to the eastern United States and southeast Canada but, unlike the black walnut, is absent frorm most of the deep south. The species is designated as "Special Concern" in Kentucky, "Exploitably Vulnerable" in New York State, and "Threatened" in Tennessee, despite the fact that it is not considered nationally threatened. The tree is often short-trunked, supporting stiff branches that form a broad open crown with a spread of 30–50 ft (9–15 m). While the soft, coarse-grained wood of the butternut is easy to work and stains and finishes well, it is more valued for its nuts than for lumber, which are prized as food by humans and animals.

INTERESTING FACTS

• Butternut shells are used in the production of grit paper, glues, plastics, and cleaning products.

• Butternut wood is used for the manufacture of flooring, furniture, musical instruments, panels, veneers, and gunstocks.

• The outer bark was used for medicinal purposes. Brewed into a tea, it was used to treat dysentery and toothaches.

HABITAT AND DISTRIBUTION

Habitat
Butternut does best on well-drained soils and stream banks and is rarely found on infertile, compact, or dry soils, although it does better than black walnut in such conditions. These trees are often found on sites with good drainage such as on slopes, stream terraces and benches, and rock ledges. In the Virginias, the tree can be found at elevations up to 4,900 ft (1,500 m), which is considerably higher than the black walnut tree.

Distribution
Juglans cinerea has a range that encompasses southern Maine to New York, west across lower Michigan to Minnesota, and south to western Virginia and North Carolina, and west to Tennessee and Missouri. In Canada, the range extends from New Brunswick to southern Quebec. It does not occur in the Deep South, unlike the black walnut.

BLACK WALNUT

Juglans nigra

Avg height: 80–120 ft (24–36 m)
Avg trunk diameter: 50–100 in (127–254 cm)
Lifespan: 150–250 years

Bark: When the tree is young, the bark is smooth and greenish-brown. As the tree ages, it turns gray and develops fractures. The bark has deep ridges and valleys.

Foliage: The leaves are thick and fernlike, providing good shade. The leaves are pinnate, containing 5–25 toothed leaflets.

Flowers: On a single tree, male and female flowers are in distinct spikes, and the female flowers usually emerge before the male. As a result, self-pollination is unlikely to occur.

Ripe nut: The fruit is a spherical nut encased in a brownish-green semifleshy husk and a brown corrugated nut, which ripens in summer and autumn and falls in October.

The eastern black walnut is a deciduous tree of the Juglandaceae family. Walnut trees thrive on soil that is wet, well-drained, and receives plenty of direct sunshine. The black walnut tree's wood has a deep dark color and is simple to work, making it a desirable commercial tree. Walnut fruits (nuts) are cultivated for their distinct taste. Walnut trees are grown for both their wood and their nuts, and a number of cultivars have been developed to provide higher-quality wood and nuts. Black walnut trees are affected by the thousand cankers disease (TCD), which has resulted in a drop in walnut tree numbers in some locations. These trees are allelopathic, as they produce toxins from their roots and other tissues that injure other organisms, giving the trees a competitive edge.

INTERESTING FACTS

• The taproots of the walnut tree are robust and deep. It generates compounds (known as juglones) that prohibit other plants from growing near the tree.

• Walnuts are high in vitamins A, E, K, and B group vitamins, as well as minerals including manganese, magnesium, phosphorus, and iron.

• Walnut fruits can be eaten as snacks or as part of a variety of desserts and salty foods.

HABITAT AND DISTRIBUTION

Habitat
Rich mesic forests, wet bottomland woodlands in valleys and along rivers, and the bases or lower slopes of bluffs are among the common habitats. The moisture-loving maple, hickory, oak, and ash trees coexist with black walnut trees in deciduous forests.

Distribution
Juglans nigra can be found from southern Ontario to southeast South Dakota, south to Georgia, northern Florida, and southwest to central Texas. It grows primarily in riparian zones.

Avg height: 30–115 ft (9–35 m)
Avg trunk diameter: 27–59 in (70–150 cm)
Lifespan: 100–500 years

Bark: The bark of young trees is smooth and yellow or orange-brown, while older trees have rough, ridged, and dark red-brown bark.

Foliage: The sassafras tree is unique in having three different shapes of leaves: unlobed, 2-lobed, and 3-lobed, and turn red in the fall.

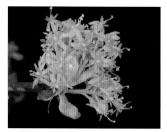

Flowers: Male and female flowers bloom on different trees. The flowers, which are 7.5 mm wide, are borne in loose clusters on 2 in (5 cm) racemes.

Seed: Sassafras drupes are dark blue or black in color and oval in form.

SASSAFRAS
Sassafras albidum

Sassafras albidum, commonly known as white or red sassafras, is a member of a genus of deciduous trees endemic to eastern North America and eastern Asia, with three living and one extinct species. Aromatic qualities characterize the genus, which has made the tree helpful to humans. The unique flavor of sassafras was originally a key component in root beer until it was discovered by the U.S. Food and Drug Administration in 1960 that safrole, a key ingredient, might be carcinogenic . On the same plant, the tree has three unique leaf shapes: unlobed oval, bilobed (mitten-shaped), and trilobed (three-pronged). Birds and animals consume the leaves, bark, twigs, stems, and fruits, and it is an important food source for deer in some areas.

INTERESTING FACTS

• Wood of sassafras is used in the manufacture of rails, cabinets, buckets, furniture, and firewood.

• Native Americans used the wood for the manufacture of canoes. They also used leaves to improve the flavor of many dishes.

• Native Americans used sassafras in the treatment of fever, diarrhea, common cold, toothache, menstrual disorders, arthritis, sore eyes, kidney problems, insect bites, nosebleeds, cuts, and sprained ankles.

HABITAT AND DISTRIBUTION

habitat
Sassafras may be found in open woodlands, along fence lines, and in fields. It thrives in moist, well-drained, or sandy loam soils and tolerates a wide range of soil types, with the best results in the southern and wetter parts of its range.

Distribution
In North America, *Sassafras albidum* may be found from southern Maine to southern Ontario, west to Iowa, and south to central Florida and eastern Texas.

Avg height: 40–80 ft (12–24 m)
Avg trunk diameter: 18–30 in (45–76 cm)
Lifespan: 200–500 years

Bark: The color of the bark is from green to reddish-brown. The young bark is smooth, thin, and gray-brown. Once the tree matures, the bark becomes scaly, thin, and continuously sheds, while the color of the bark darkens to brown.

Foliage: The dark green foliage is thick and leathery, shiny above and dull and lighter below. The simple, pinnate leaves are alternate, and elliptical to lanceolate, with smooth margins, 1.2–4 in (3–10 cm) long and 0.6–1.2 in (1.5–3 cm) broad. They are an irritant to the nose and eyes when crushed.

Flowers: The flowers are yellow to green and occur in clusters, each of which contains 4–9 flowers, which grow on the stem. Abundant fruits occur after 30–40 years. These fruits, also known as "California bay nuts," are round green berries 0.8–1 in (2–2.5 cm) long and 0.8 in (2 cm) wide. They are lightly spotted with yellow and turn purple once mature.

CALIFORNIA LAUREL
Umbellularia californica

Umbellularia californica, also known as California laurel, is an evergreen tree belonging to the family Lauraceae, native to the Pacific Coast of North America. The speed and size of growth largely depend on the local conditions. This plant releases terpenes that kill any competing plants and therefore can limit the germination of plants nearby. It often grows in gardens and along waterways, therefore storing stream channels. The plant has short-stalked, alternate smooth-edged leaves which are oval or oblong. These leaves give off a pungent scent when crushed. They grow in partial shades or full sun and occupy a great variety of habitats. California laurel leaves are rich in proteins and are a good food source for deer, while the branches are often used as nesting sites for a variety of birds.

INTERESTING FACTS

· The leaves of the California laurel were often used by people to rid themselves of fleas and headlice. Scientists have studied the plant and found that the dusky-footed woodrat uses the leaves of the laurel to keep fleas out of its nests.

· An infusion of the leaves was used to treat intestinal cramps and neuralgia.

· The seeds of the plant can be ground into a powder to be used along with cereal flours to make bread.

HABITAT AND DISTRIBUTION

Habitat
The California laurel grows in an extremely diverse range of climates, from cool, humid environments in dense coastal areas to dry, hot atmospheres such as open woods and scrublands. It was recorded that the tree can tolerate extreme temperatures as low as -13° and as high as 118°F (-25° to 48°C).

Distribution
In the north, the California laurel ranges from southwest Oregon to southern California. Isolated stands can also be found in Washington and coastal British Columbia. The tree commonly occurs at an altitude of 5,249 ft (1,600 m) above sea level.

HONEYLOCUST
Gleditsia triacanthos

Avg height: 66–98 ft (20–30 m)
Avg trunk diameter: 24–36 in (60–91 cm)
Lifespan: 100–150 years

Bark: The bark is gray-brown to reddish-brown, changing slightly to bronze with age. The bark of a young tree is smooth with several horizontal lenticels that change to long, narrow, curling plates over time.

Foliage: The leaves are broad, pinnate when young, and bipinnate once matured. They are alternately arranged around the stem. They are dark green before changing to a golden yellow before falling.

Flowers: The flowers are green-white and small, in groups at leaf axils. Some flowers may have both male and female parts.

Fruit: The fruit is a flat reddish-brown pod nearly 18 in (45 cm) long, sickle-shaped, and twisted, with a sweet-tasting pulp.

Gleditsia triacanthos, also known as honeylocust, thorny honeylocust, or thorny locust, belongs to the family Fabaceae. The common names result from the clusters of sharp, thorny branches. The deciduous tree is often found in moist soil close to river valleys. It is able to adapt to a range of environments and is considered an aggressive invasive species. The pulp of the tree's pods is widely consumed by wildlife and livestock. The wood of the honeylocust is high-quality and polishes well, although the relative scarcity of the tree makes it insufficient to support the bulk of the lumber industry. There is, however, a separate market that is specific to furniture made from honeylocust lumber.

INTERESTING FACTS

• The dispersion of seeds is achieved by grazing herbivores because the digestive enzyme present in their guts softens the coat of the seeds and enhances germination.

• The wood of honeylocust is a popular option for firewood and can also be converted to ethanol that can be used as biofuel.

• The honeylocust is also known as the confederate pintree because its formidable thorns were used to pin together the uniforms of confederate soldiers during the American civil war.

HABITAT AND DISTRIBUTION

Habitat
Honeylocusts often grow in moist soil near river valleys and in plain open areas. As long as it receives suitable sunlight, the honeylocust can survive in both urban and suburban environments, although it prefers alluvial flood plains. It is drought-tolerant and has no major problems with pests or disease.

Distribution
The range of the honeylocust extends from central Pennsylvania to southern Ontario, southern Michigan, southern Wisconsin, southern South Dakota, south through eastern Nebraska to eastern Texas, then east Alabama and along the western slope of the Appalachians. Isolated stands can also be found in northwest Florida.

KENTUCKY COFFEETREE
Gymnocladus dioicus

Avg height: 60–75 ft (18–22.8 m)
Avg trunk diameter: 24–36 in (60–90 cm)
Lifespan: 100–150 years

Bark: The bark of a young tree is gray with flaky scales that curl outward at the edges. On a mature tree, the bark is a dark brownish-gray color and develops deep fissures with rough, scaly ridges.

Foliage: The leaves of the Kentucky coffeetree are binately pinnate and very large, reaching 12–36 in (30–90 cm) in length and 18–24 in (45–60 cm) in width. When they initially sprout from the bud they are bright pink but turn green over time, dark yellow-green above and pale green below.

Flowers and fruit: The Kentucky coffeetree is dioecious so the female flowers and later the fruits are only on one tree. The fruits are legumes, leathery curved pods of 6–10 in (15–25 cm) long and 1.5–2 in (3.8–5 cm) wide with 6–9 seeds. The seed pods must rot in order for the seeds to be released to germinate.

The Kentucky coffeetree belongs to the subfamily of Caesalpinioideae, which is native to the central United States and southern Canada. The crown is narrow and pyramidal when receiving adequate light; when crowded by other trees, the trunk may be branchless for up to 70 ft (21 m). It was the Kentucky state tree from 1976–1994, when it was replaced by the tulip poplar. It is a popular wood for use by carpenters and cabinet makers. As the tree is relatively fast-growing, it is often used as a decorative tree on city streets and in parks. The seeds are sometimes used as a substitute for coffee beans although they are poisonous if not roasted. The seed pods are too tough for most wildlife to consume, so the distribution of seeds is limited to flowing water, resulting in the Kentucky coffeetree now being considered a rare species in spite of its wide distribution.

INTERESTING FACTS

• Native tribes used the seeds as dice in games of chance, as well as in their jewelry as decorative items.

• The wood of the coffeetree is rot-resistant and was, therefore, a popular choice for fence posts and railroad ties.

• The Kentucky coffeetree is one of three species in the genus *Gymnocladus*, the other two being native to eastern Asia, specifically in China and Myanmar..

HABITAT AND DISTRIBUTION

Habitat
The Kentucky coffeetree can often be found in river valleys and floodplains and occasionally in limestone woods and on rocky hillsides.

Distribution
The Kentucky coffeetree is a rare tree species, in spite of its wide distribution range. It can be found in the United States from northern Louisiana to southern Wisconsin and Michigan, to southeastern South Dakota, eastern Nebraska, and Kansas, and to Kentucky and Connecticut. In Canada, it can be found in southern Ontario.

HONEY MESQUITE

Prosopis glandulos

Avg height: 20–30 ft (6–9 m)
Avg trunk diameter: 12–18 in (30–45 cm)
Lifespan: 40– 120 years

Bark: The bark of a young tree is gray with flaky scales which curl outward at the edges. On a mature tree, the bark is dark brownish-gray and develops deep fissures with rough, scaly ridges.

Foliage: Leaves are deciduous and twice-compound. They are bright green and feathery, with leaflets up to 2 in (5 cm) long and 3.2 in (8 cm) wide.

Flowers: The tree flowers from March to November with tiny, pale yellow flowers occurring in dense racemes. The flowers are fragrant and attract pollinators. Fruit occurs as a long, yellow-brown pod, somewhat flattened with slight constrictions between the seeds, making them very distinct.

Prosopis glandulosa, also known as honey mesquite, is a small flowering tree in the legume family of Fabaceae. The crown is rounded and crooked, made up of branches that are rounded and floppy, sporting feathery foliage. While it is native to the southwestern United States and Mexico, it has been introduced to at least six other countries and is considered by the IUCN to be one of the world's 100 worst invasive species. In the Central Valley of California, however, it serves an important role as a habitat plant for many species of wildlife. It has been used by different indigenous tribes for a variety of purposes: The Pueblo peoples make their horno bread using mesquite flour that is made from honey mesquite seeds, while the Cahuilla people ground the pods into meal to make cake, as well as eating the blossoms.

INTERESTING FACTS

• The honey mesquite provides excellent shelter and nest-building materials for wildlife while the seed pods are produced in abundance, serving as a food source for diverse small mammal and bird species.

• The tree is a honey plant and supports native species of bees as well as cultivated honey bees. It is also a larval host for Reakirt's blue butterflies and the long-tailed skipper.

• Parts of the plant were used medicinally by indigenous peoples of southwestern North America and California, as well as for fuel and making tools and arrowheads.

HABITAT AND DISTRIBUTION

Habitat
The honey mesquite is highly adapted to arid environments and has a very deep taproot, which can reach up to 100 ft (30 m) in order to reach underground water. The honey mesquite is often found in coastal prairies, deserts, arroyos, grasslands, plains, and plateaus, where the soil tends to be dry and the sunlight is plentiful.

Distribution
While primarily native to northern Mexico and the southwestern U.S., the honey mesquite extends its range from California east to Kansas and south to Louisiana, Nuevo Leon, and Baja California. It can also be found in southwestern Kansas, Nevada, western Oklahoma, most of Texas, New Mexico, and Louisiana, as well as Coahuila and Tamaulipas in Mexico.

Avg height: 40–100 ft (12–30 m)
Avg trunk diameter: 24-48 in (61–121 cm)
Lifespan: 50–100 yrs

Bark: The bark is light brown and rough; with age, it is increasingly wrinkled, darker brown, and heavily furrowed with deep grooves and ridges forming thin diamond-shaped platelets in the bark.

Foliage: Each compound leaf has 9–21 leaflets, which are 1–2 in (2.5–5 cm) long and 0.25–0.75 in (0.6–1.9 cm) wide.

Flowers: The flowers open in May or June and are creamy-white with a pale yellow blotch in the center. Each individual flower is about 1 in (2.5 cm) wide, and grow in drooping racemes 4–8 in (10–20 cm) long. They are fragrant, producing large amounts of nectar, and are pollinated by insects..

Spines: Black locusts have pairs of thorns at the base of each leaf rather than the long thorns of the honey locust.

BLACK LOCUST
Robinia pseudoacacia

Robinia pseudoacacia, also known as black locust, or false acacia, after its species name "pseudoacacia," is one of the toughest hardwoods in North America. It is a fast-growing, medium-sized deciduous tree native to the eastern U.S. The black locust belongs to the Faboideae, which is part of the legume family Fabaceae, and is a relative of the bean and pea. It is a prolific grower and, through shading open habitats, it converts a grassland ecosystem into a forested ecosystem and displaces the grasses. It is listed as invasive in Connecticut and Wisconsin and is forbidden in Massachusetts. Although *Robinia* is native to North America, fossilized traces of it have been found in Eocene and Miocene rocks in Europe. Although the seeds are edible, the bark, leaves, and wood are toxic to both humans and livestock.

INTERESTING FACTS

• The black locust helped build Jamestown which is where the tree was identified in 1607 by British colonists, who built their houses from the timber.

• The strength of the black locust lumber hardened the navy that decided the outcome of the War of 1812.

• The heartwood of the black locust tree is resistant to rot and produces dense, heavy wood.

• The nectar from the blooms is essential for bees and results in excellent quality honey.

HABITAT AND DISTRIBUTION

Habitat
The black locust is intolerant to shade and as such is typical of disturbed areas and young woodlands where the soil is dry and sunlight is plentiful. The black locust does inhabit a broad range of conditions and forest types, however.

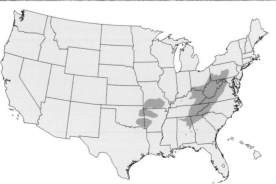

Distribution
While *Robinia pseudoacacia* is native to eastern North America, its exact native range is unknown. It can be found in all the lower 48 states, eastern Canada, and British Columbia. It is hypothesized that the native range was two separate populations, one focusing around the Appalachian Mountains and the other focusing around the Ozark Plateau and Ouachita Mountains of Missouri, Arkansas, and Oklahoma.

HARDWOOD LEAVES AND FRUIT:
PALMATE AND PINNATELY COMPOSITE LEAVES

Leaf shape is probably the easiest way to identify a tree, although not always the most reliable because of the great variation within and among species. The most common forms in the hardwood trees are palmate single, with several veins branching off at the base of the leaf at its connection with the stem; pinnate single, with a single vein, off which pairs of veins branch from the base to the tip of the leaf; and pinnately compound leaves, having pinnate leaflets coming off the primary vein. Fruits is also used to distinguish among trees; for many, the combination of tree and fruit can be conclusive.

Sweetgum *Liquidambar styraciflua*
The palmate leaves are star-shaped, with five to seven pointed lobes The spherical compound fruit is composed of 40–60 individual capsules, each with one or two seeds and a pair of terminal spikes. When these .capsules are released, a small hole remains in the fruit.

Sassafras *Sassafras albidum*
Noted for its varied leaves—three-lobed and two-lobed as well as unlobed, eliptical leaves, arranged alternately all on the same branch. The fruit of the Sassafrass is a blue-black berry that contains a single seed, on a red pedicel.

American Sycamore *Platanus occidentalis*
The palmate leaves have 3–5 lobes and coarse marginal teeth. The fruiting balls are composed of densely packed tiny seedlike fruits, and the balls disintegrate as the seeds are released in the fall

Black Walnut *Juglans nigra*
The binately compound leaves are arranged alternately, dark above and hairy underneath. The largest leaflets are at the center of the leaf, and are serrated. The spherical fruit, which ripens during the summer and autumn and falls in October, is a nut with a brownish-green husk and a brown, corrugated nut; the seed within is small and very hard..

Honeylocust *Gleditsiz triacanthos*
The leaves are bipinnately compound; the leaflets are darker green on the upper side than the lower. The long flat pods are edible by humans and are eaten by ranch animals and other grazing herbivores, which consume the honeylike pulp while breaking down the seed coats in their digestive system and releasing the seeds in their droppings.

Kentucky Coffeetree *Gymnocladus dioicus*
The leaves are bipinnately compound and can reach over 3 ft (91 cm) long and 2 ft (61 cm) wide; the bottom pair are leaflets and the other seven to thirteen pairs are foliate. The fruit is a reddish-brown pod, with 6–9 seeds encased in a rich pulp.

Honey Mesquite *Prosopis glandulosa*
The feathery pinnately compound leaves have a single pair of major leaflets, each with 10–20 pairs of narrow subleaflets. The seeds are disseminated by the livestock grazing on the sweet bean pods

Black Locust *Robinia pseudoacacia*
There is one leaflet at the tip of the compound leaf, and all of the leaflets are rounded. The small dark pods are flat with 4–8 seeds surrounded by a pulp; they ripen in late fall but are not shed until spring. They are **poisonous** to humans, horses, and cattle, unlike the long pods of the Honeylocust, which can be identified by their narrow leaflets.

YELLOW POPLAR
Liriodendron tulipifera

Avg height: 80–100 ft (24–30 m)
Avg trunk diameter: 48–72 in (60–182 cm)
Lifespan: 200–300 years

Bark: Young trees have smooth, dark green bark. As the tree matures, wide white furrows appear, splitting the bark into flat ridges. When young, the bark is gray and thin, with the color darkening and the texture becoming coarser over time.

Leaves and flowers: The pinnate leaves have 4–6 lobes separated by rounded notches, up to 6 in (15 cm) long, with four distinct points. The flowers, which are perfect, open in May, and are solitary and terminal

Fruit: The fruit is a cone-shaped collection of many winged seeds or samaras, which is dry, oblong, scaly, and brown. The seeds are dispersed by the wind in late fall and winter, remaining viable for 4–7 years after falling. The axis stays on the tree through the winter.

Liriodendron tulipifera, also known as yellow poplar, tuliptree, tulip-poplar, white-poplar, and whitewood, is a deciduous eastern hardwood with a single straight trunk and a narrow pyramidal crown that widens as the tree ages. The yellow poplar is the tallest hardwood tree in North America. The tree is named for its flowers, which are showy and resemble tulips, and *liriodendron* means "lily tree" in Greek. The leaves resemble maple and other palmate leaves in shape and turn brilliant yellow in fall, but they are pinnate, with just a single main vein. The wood of the yellow poplar was commonly hollowed out for use dugout canoes and today is used for making pallets and building furniture.

INTERESTING FACTS

• Yellow poplar is valued as a shade tree for large areas, as a source of wildlife food, and as a honey tree.

• The wood of the tulip poplar is a favorite for wood carving by sculptors, including Shields Landon Jones and Wilhelm Schimmel.

• The yellow poplar has been referenced in literature, including William Stafford's poem "Tulip Tree" and Edgar Allan Poe's short story "The Gold-Bug."

HABITAT AND DISTRIBUTION

Habitat
As the yellow poplar is widely distributed, it can grow under a variety of climate conditions. Within the north-south range of the yellow poplar, temperature extremes vary from 19°–81°F (-7.2°–27.2°C), while rainfall can vary from 30–80 in (760–2,030 mm) annually and frost-free days vary from 150 to more that 310.

Distribution
The yellow poplar can be found from north-central Florida west to Louisiana, north to Michigan and southern Ontario, and east through southern New England. The tree reaches its largest size and is most abundant in the valley of the Ohio River and on the mountain slopes of West Virginia, Kentucky, Tennessee, and North Carolina.

SOUTHERN MAGNOLIA
Magnolia grandiflora

Avg height: 60–80 ft (18–24 m)
Avg trunk diameter: 24–36 in (61–91 cm)
Lifespan: 80–120 years

Bark: The gray to brown bark is thin and smooth with lenticels when young, developing close plates or scales with age.

Leaves: Very thick, waxy dark green leaves are simple and pinnately veined, oval to elliptical, 5–8 in (8–20 cm) long, and are paler with a rusty fuzz on the underside.

Flowers: Citronella-scented white flowers, 6–8 in (15–20 cm) wide with 6–15 petal-like tepals from April to June. They are perfect: they have both male and female parts.

Fruit: The fused aggregate of follicles 3–5 in (7.5–12.7 cm) long is brown when mature in fall. Bright red seed 0.5 in (1.3 cm) long in each follicle.

Magnolia grandiflora, also known as southern magnolia, evergreen magnolia, bull-bay, big-laurel, or large-flower magnolia. The magnolia is evergreen, dropping leaves throughout the year from the inside of the crown; these leaves, since they are so heavy, cover the soil. However, most leaves remain on the tree until they are replaced new foliage in the spring. Linnaeaus gave the tree its scientific name, *Magnolia* after the French botanist Magnol, and *grandiflora* from the Latin words "grandis" (big) and "flor" (flower). The Cherokees and other native american tribes used various parts of the magnolia to make infusions to use medicinally. An infusion of the bark was used for stomachache or cramps, or held in the mouth to treat toothache.

INTERESTING FACTS

• Quail, turkeys, squirrels and opossums, eat the drupes; the seeds are then dispersed, but some seeds may be dispersed by heavy rains as well ."

• Two of the biggest southern magnolias have grown in the far south of their range, where the temperatures are the warmest.

• One giant, 121 ft (37 m), was found in Smith County, Mississippi; another, 98 ft (30 m) and 18 ft (5.5 m) in circumference, was found in Baton Rouge, Louisiana.,

HABITAT AND DISTRIBUTION

Habitat
Southern magnolia grows best in rich, moist, well-drained soils of bottoms and low uplands. and is endemic to evergreen lowland subtropial forests. Although it can be found along streams and near swamps, and in wooded floodplains, it cannot tolerate continual flooding.

Distribution
The southern magnolia is native only to the coastal plains of the southeast Atlantic Coast, from North Carolina south to Florida, and west across the southern half of Georgia, Alabama,Mississippi, Louisiana, and into southeast Texas.

Avg height: 40–60 ft (12–18 m)
Avg trunk diameter: 48–72 in (60–182 cm)
Lifespan: 80–120 years

Bark: Young trees have a smooth and green bark, but as the tree matures the trunk becomes silvery gray and is often mottled.

Leaves: Aromatic spicy leaves are laurel-like, silvery below, elliptical to oblong-lanceolate, shiny, 3–6 in (7.5–15 cm) long, and 1–3 in (2.5–7.5 cm) wide.

Flowers: Vanilla-scented white blooms from mid-spring sporadically into summer months: 9–12 petals; 1–3 in (2.5–7.5 cm).

Fruit: The fused aggregate of follicles 1.2–2 in (3–5 cm) long is pinkish-red when mature. The follicles split open to release 10 mm long black seeds, covered by a fleshy red coat.

SWEETBAY
Magnolia virginiana

Magnolia virginiana is most commonly known as sweetbay magnolia, or merely sweetbay, but also as laurel magnolia, swampbay, swamp magnolia, whitebay, or beaver tree. The common name comes from the sweet-smelling, baylike foliage. Under the modern rules of botanical nomenclature, *M. virginiana* was the first species of the genus *Magnolia* to be described and is therefore the type species of *Magnolia*; likewise, *Magnolia* was the first genus of flowering plants to be described; therefore, *Magnolia virginiana* is the "type species" for all flowering plants. The sweetbay is the host plant for the larvae of the spicebush swallowtail, eastern tiger swallowtail, and palamedes swallowtail butterflies, and sweetbay silkmoth; the butterflies lay their eggs on the branches, and when the larvae hatch, they feed on the leaves.

INTERESTING FACTS

• Although sweetbay is generally deer-resistant, white-tailed deer may nibble on the sweet leaves or twigs on occasion.

• In addition to being a larval host plant for several species of butterflies, many more are attracted to the sweet-smelling blossoms.

• In fall, squirrels, rodents, bobwhites, and turkeys are attracted to the red fruits when they fall down to the ground. Other birds that are attracted to the fruit include blue jays, flickers, towhees, and vireos.

HABITAT AND DISTRIBUTION

Habitat
The sweetbay prefers wet, swampy sites such as waterlogged forests and along stream banks, and requires acidice soils. It is moderately salt-tolerant. It provides cover from winter weather and extreme conditions.

Distribution
The sweetbay is native to the Atlanic Coast from New York south to the tip of Florida, and west along the Gulf states from Florida, Georgia, Alabama, and Mississippi, through to southeastern Texas, as well as north from Louisiana and Mississippi into southern Arkansas and Tennessee.

OSAGE ORANGE
Maclura pomifera

Avg height: 30–65 ft (9–20 m)
Avg trunk diameter: 12–20 in (30.5–51 cm)
Lifespan: 100–150 years

Bark: When young, the tree has a bright orange bark that turns scaly, dark, and deeply furrowed once it matures.

Foliage: The leaves are 3–5 inches (8–13 cm) long and 2–3 inches (5–8 cm) wide. The foliage is a thick, shining dark green with a paler green underneath, turning yellow in fall.

Flowers: Flowers usually occur from April to June. Male flowers are small and pale green with a hairy, four–lobed calyx and slender long drooping peduncles. Female flowers occur in many–flowered heads and are dense.

Fruit: The fruit ripens in September and October. It is 4–5 inches (13–15 cm) in diameter and looks like a yellow-green orange with a rough surface.

Maclura pomifera, also known as Osage orange, horse apple, hedge apple tree, or hedge, grows either as a large shrub or as a small tree. The tree trunk is short with a rounded crown. This tree was first identified by Scottish explorer William Dunbar, in 1804. It earned its name "Osage" because it was utilized by the Osage Native Americans. It was called "Hedge" by American settlers because it was used as a natural barrier to keep livestock from cornfields and vegetable gardens. The French called it "bois d'arc" (which translates to bow–wood) because when they first settled in America, they said the Native Americans used the wood of this tree for making bows and clubs. This is also what originated the names "bodock," "bodark," or "bodarc" for these trees. The wood of this tree was in very high demand for its strength, durability, and flexibility.

INTERESTING FACTS

• The demand for the wood of this tree was so high that people were willing to travel hundreds of miles for it. It has the highest recorded wood density and highest burn temperature recorded for trees.

• The wood of this tree was used for making fences, hubs, wooden stoves, wheel rims for horse-drawn carriages, posts, and mine-support timber.

• No animal has been recorded to be able to digest its fruit completely.

HABITAT AND DISTRIBUTION

Habitat
This tree can adapt to many soil conditions but it grows best in full sun. It can be cultivated in dry, wet, alkaline, clayey, shallow, sandy, or poor soils, although it prefers rich and moist soils. It will tolerate cool temperatures and 40–45 in (100–115 cm) of rain annually but it is sensitive to extreme cold.

Distribution
The natural range of the osage orange is a very small and restricted area of the U.S. that includes a corner of Arkansas, the Chiso mountains of Texas, Red River drainage of Oklahoma, post oak savannas, and Blackland Prairies. It is also cultivated in Ontario, Canada.

Avg height: 60–80 ft (18.25–25.25 m)
Avg trunk diameter: 20–39 in (50–100 cm)
Lifespan: 500–700 years

BLACK TUPELO
Nyssa sylvatica

Nyssa sylvatica, also known as black tupelo, American black gum, or sour gum, or merely tupelo, has a straight trunk with branches extending outward at right angles, forming a crown that is pyramidal when young, becoming rounded as it matures. This tree is tolerant of poorly drained soils and can grow in standing water. The black tupelo flowers are an important source of nectar for bees and their fruits are a food source for many mammals and birds. These trees are often cultivated as ornamental trees in large gardens and parks. Because its wood is heavy and resistant to wear, it has been a favorite for diverse uses from railroad ties and factory floors to pulleys, bowls, and loom shuttles for weaving.

INTERESTING FACTS

• The genus name comes from a Greek water nymph Nyssa or Nysa and the species, *sylvatica*, means wood.

• The common name "tupelo" is Native American in origin, coming from the Creek words *ito* meaning "tree" and *opilwa* meaning "swamp."

• Hollow trunks of the black tupelo provide denning or nesting opportunities for various mammals and bees.

Bark: When young, the bark is flaky and dark gray. With age, it becomes furrowed and on very old stems will resemble alligator hide.

Foliage: Leaves are alternately arranged and dark green above and paler below. They can be a variety of shapes and sizes, including obovate, elliptical, or oval, and range from 2–4.5 in (5–12 cm) in length. In the fall, they turn a spectacular scarlet color.

Flowers: The black tupelo flowers, while not showy, are an excellent source of nectar for bees. The flowers are small and greenish–white with the female flowers growing in sparse clusters and the male flowers in dense heads.

Fruit: Flowers give way to fruit which are around 0.5 in (1.25 cm) long and oval. These fruits are edible but sour, maturing to a dark blue that is attractive to wildlife.

HABITAT AND DISTRIBUTION

Habitat
This tree is primarily a lowland tree and is found in pond peripheries, bottomlands, and low wet woods. It can also grow on ravines and dry rocky wooded slopes. It grows best in moist woodland gardens, naturalized areas, boggy areas, or low areas subject to periodic flooding.

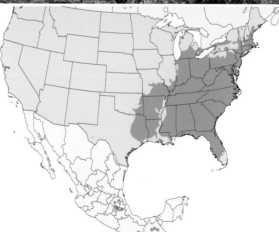

Distribution
Nyssa sylvatica is native to eastern North America and can be found from southern Florida, eastern Texas, and eastern Oklahoma north to central Missouri, Illinois, central Michigan, extreme southern Ontario, New York, and southwestern Maine. It can also be found in central and southern Mexico.

AMERICAN ASH
Fraxinus americana

Avg height: 60–120 ft (18–36.5 m)
Avg trunk diameter: 24–36 in (61–91 cm)
Lifespan: 200–300 years

Bark: The bark is yellow–brown to a light gray or silvery brown. It is corky with deep furrows and short, pointed, diamond–shaped ridges.

Foliage: The leaves are pinnately compound with 5–9 (most often 7) leaflets. They are ovate, obovate, oblong, or lanceolate with smooth or partially serrated margins, and 8–12 in (20–30.5 cm) long. The leaflets are 3–5 in (7.5–12.75 cm) long and are dark green above and whitish-green below.

Flowers and fruit: Male and female flowers may appear on different trees or the same. Flowers appear in April or May and persist 2–3 weeks before falling. Early flowers measure 3–4 in (20–25 cm) wide while fully developed flowers can be 8–10 in (20–25 cm) wide. The flowers are light green to purple and lack petals. Fruits usually contain only one seed or rarely two. Fruits are clusters of winged samara that usually droop.

Fraxinus americana, also known as American ash or white ash, is a member of a genus with representatives across Europe, Asia, and North America. Both the genus name of *Fraxinus* and the common name, ash, are used for "spear" because ash wood has been used for spear shafts. It is one of the most popular landscaping species and supports a wide variety of uses. It is a vital food source for North American frogs and, also, the tadpoles, which feed on the leaves whether in ponds or merely temporary puddles. The crown becomes rounded with age and has a pyramidal to an upright oval shape when the tree is young. Seedeating birds such as cedar waxwings, cardinals, and pine grosbeaks eat ash seeds, as do voles and other rodents. Deer eat the foliage, and some birds and small mammals nest in ash trees.

INTERESTING FACTS

• The wood of this tree is used for baseball bats, oars, polo mallets, tennis racquets, hockey sticks, furniture, flooring, tool handles, and playground equipment.

• The wood of the American ash has high antibacterial properties determined by a comparative study with eight other tree species, making it a good choice for cutting boards.

• The emerald ash borers are able to kill an American ash tree in 3–5 years and have become a severe threat to the species' survival since the late 1980s, when they were introduced accidentally into North America.

HABITAT AND DISTRIBUTION

Habitat
This plant grows in a diverse range of climates from 7ºF to 81ºF (–14ºC to 27ºC) with an average annual rainfall of 60 in (152.5 cm). It needs highly fertile soils to grow with a substantial nitrogen content and a calcium content that is moderate to high. It can grow from near sea level to an elevation of 3,450 ft (1,050 m).

Distribution
This plant grows from Nova Scotia and Cape Breton Island, west to eastern Minnesota, south to northern Florida, and southwest to eastern Texas at the westernmost part of its range. It has also been found in Hawaii, Wyoming, Colorado, and North Carolina. It has been cultivated in the Cumberland Mountains, New York's Adirondack Mountains, and the southeastern coastal plain.

AMERICAN SYCAMORE
Platanus occidentalis

Avg height: 75–175 ft (23–53 m)
Avg trunk diameter: 3–8 ft (91–244 cm)
Lifespan: 250–300 years

Bark: The bark of this tree is dark reddish-brown with oblong platelike scales. The bark changes to a light gray higher up on the tree and peels off in thin strips, revealing a pale yellow, white or greenish surface.

Foliage and fruit: The leaves are 4–9 in (10–23 cm) long, arranged alternately with 3–5 lobes and toothed margins, and are wedge-shaped at the base. The brown, ball-like fruits are 1 in (2.5 cm) in diameter and hang alone on stalks 3–6 in (7.5–15 cm) long. Each tiny seed is in a separate capsule that is carried in the air by hairlike fibers, or they may be consumed by small small animals.

Platanus occidentalis, also known as American sycamore, American planetree, western plane, occidental plane, buttonwood, and water beech, is a tree native to the eastern and central U.S. Carl Linnaeus derived its name "occidentalis" from the Latin word meaning "western," as opposed to the Oriental plane, *Platanus orientalis*, which was native in the Eastern Hemisphere, from the Balkans to Iran. The London plane tree was formed by accidental hybridization in the 17th century when an American sycamore and an Oriental plane happened to have been planted close to each other, and the hybrid was fertile. It can easily be distinguished from other trees by its physical characteristics, including its mottled bark flaking off in irregular pieces.

INTERESTING FACTS

• This species is often used for shade in big cities as it is resistant to pollution and urban conditions so it is a very common street tree. It has also been used as a biomass crop.

• Sycamores can reach enormous proportions. One of the best known is the "Buttonball Tree" in Sunderland, Massachusetts, more than 113 ft (34 m) high, with a circumference of 25 ft 8 in (8 m).

• In 1744, a man and his two sons lived for most of a year in a hollow sycamore in Virginia.

HABITAT AND DISTRIBUTION

Habitat
This tree is commonly found in wetland and riparian areas. It grows best on average well-drained soils that are medium wet. Rich and consistently moist soils are ideal. It can withstand light shade but prefers full sun. It can resist damage from most urban pollutants, deer, drought, wet soils, and wind.

Distribution
Its range extends to Nebraska in the west, New Hampshire in the north, from Iowa to Ontario, and to the south of Texas and Florida. It used to be found in Maine but is now extinct there. Successful plantations of this tree have been found in Bismarck, North Dakota, and Okeechobee.

Flowers: The flowers bloom at the same time that leaves emerge in May; the female flowers are in dense clusters that later form the fruiting balls. Although the tree is monoecious, the pollen from male flowers fertilizes the female flowers of another tree.

DOWNY SERVICEBERRY
Amelanchier arborea

Avg height: 20–30 ft (6–9 m)
Avg trunk diameter: 4–6 in (10–15 cm)
Lifespan: 40–60 years

Bark: The bark is smooth overall and usually gray with darker stripes. As it ages, it becomes rough and has vertical splits and furrows.

Flowers: Showy, slightly fragrant, white flowers appear before the leaves emerge in early spring. They are perfect with 5 petals and grow in drooping clusters of 4–10 flowers 0.5–1 in (4–8 cm) wide. The flowers are pollinated by bees.

Foliage and fruit: The obovate and finely toothed leaves have pointed tips and are 1.5–3.25 in (4–8 cm) long and 1–1.5 in (2.5–4 cm) wide. In the fall, the colors vary from reddish or pinkish to orange–yellow. The fruits are small, round berries that are initially green and turn red and eventually a dark purple–black color.

Amelanchier arborea, also known as serviceberry, downy serviceberry, juneberries, shadberry, service or sarvice berry, and common serviceberry, is a deciduous small tree or large shrub. This tree comes from the Rosaceae, the rose family. There are a lot of different species of this tree, which can be hard to identify because of their similarities, however, the "downy" in its common name refers to the underside of the young leaves when they emerge in the spring. These trees are short and airy with some being classified as shrubs. Noted for its merits as a landscape plant, this tree has beautiful fall colors and its white spring flowers produce fruit that is greatly enjoyed by a broad range of wildlife, particularly birds.

INTERESTING FACTS

• The roots of the serviceberry are not invasive, allowing other plants to grow close to the base of the tree.

• The bark is susceptible to damage by pests and disease, causing wood decay and types of rust.

• It is possible that the root of the name "serviceberry" comes from the blooming of the tree's flowers coinciding with the roads opening in the Appalachian mountains, allowing preachers to travel and communities to have Sunday services again.

• The downy serviceberry was used by Native Americans to make bread.

HABITAT AND DISTRIBUTION

Habitat
The downy serviceberry commonly occurs in open rocky woods, bluffs, and wooded slopes. It tolerates varying levels of light but grows best in full sun.

Distribution
The downy serviceberry can be found from the Gulf Coast north to Lake St. John in Quebec and Thunder Bay in Ontario, and west to Minnesota and Texas.

Avg height: 15–30 ft (4.5–9 m)
Avg trunk diameter: 6–12 in (15–30 cm)
Lifespan: 50–100 years

Bark: The bark is variable in color, often reddish gray–brown and occasionally dark gray or dark brown. It is rough in texture and is covered with longitudinal scales.

Foliage and fruit: The leaves are cuneate, elliptical, or lanceolate in shape, and coarsely toothed. Alternately arranged, they are 1.5–3 in (4–8 cm) long and 1–1.5 in (2.5–4 cm) wide, and yellow-green in color, with pale green undersurface. The fruits, which are yellow–green or yellow once mature, persist from September to October. They are 0.75–1.5 in (2–3.75 cm) across and are fragrant and slightly sour, with a fleshy white fruit.

Flowers: The flowers, which are perfect, appear in May in clusters of 2–6. Individual flowers are 1–1.75 in (2.5–4.5 cm) across and have 5 pink petals that fade to white over time.

SWEET CRAB APPLE
Malus coronoria

Malus coronaria, also known as wild crabapple, sweet crabapple, garland crab, and American crabapple, is a small deciduous tree belonging to the rose family. One of the botanists who described the crab apple for Linnaeus, Pehr Kalm, reported that, although the crab apples lie under the trees all winter, they don't start to rot until spring. Linnaeaus gave the tree its species name, *coronaria*, meaning garland, in reference to its perfume. It has a short trunk that is often crooked and a broad, open crown that in spring is covered in fragrant pink flowers. The tree is often used by wildlife as a nesting site, for cover, and as a food source. It was used by the Iroquois and other Native American peoples for food and medicines, and by early settlers for grist mills and tool handles.

INTERESTING FACTS

• The fruits are a food source for foxes, squirrels, opossums, rabbits, raccoons, and a variety of birds, while the branches provide cover and nesting sites for small mammals and birds.

• While the fruit is somewhat sour, it can be made into ciders and preserves.

• The tree is very valuable to a variety of bees, including bumble bees, long–horned bees, short–tongued bees, and honey bees.

HABITAT AND DISTRIBUTION

Habitat
The sweet crabapple prefers moist, loamy soil in full sun but will tolerate partial shade. In the southern end of its range, it is commonly found in mountains. It grows will in woodland edges, open woods, and stream banks.

Distribution
The sweet crab apple is native to the Great Lakes region and the Ohio Valley, concentrated in southern Michigan, Indiana, and Ohio, but there are disjunct populations as far South Carolina, eastern Tennessee, and Long Island, New York.

HARDWOOD LEAVES AND FRUIT: SIMPLE PINNATE

There is a wide variety among leaves that are defined as simple and pinnate and, also, among their fruits. Leaves are termed pinnate as opposed to palmate if they have just one vein that goes the full length of the leaf from its base to its tip, with all other veins branching off that one rather than coming up from the base. In most leaves, this is obvious, although exceptions exist. Yellow Poplar leaves look much like maple leaves but the veins to their lobes branch off a main vein rather than out of the base of the leaf.

Simple leaves have just one leaf off that vein, whereas compound leaves have pinnate leaflets coming off the main vein rather than just veins. As with the other hardwoods, the fruit forms include samura, nuts, berries, catkins, and drupes.

Yellow Poplar (Tuliptree)
Liriodendron tulipifera
The leaves are pinnate but four-lobed and appear so similar to maple leaves that they look palmate. The fruit is formed from an upright cluster of light brown samaras that unfold and drop their seeds in the winter.

California Laurel
Umbellularia californica
The evergreen pinnate leaves are smooth-edged and lance-shaped. The fruit is a round green berry approximately an inch (2.5 cm) in diameter, which ripens in October–November. The hard, thin-shelled pit is enclosed in an oily, fleshy covering within a thin, leathery skin.

Osage Orange
Maclura pomifera
The leaves are long, oval, and have a sharp tip. They are dark green and shining above, and lighter green underneath. The fruit is an aggregate of drupes produced by hundreds of flowers that have grown together.

Black Tupelo
Nyssa sylvatica
Waxy, dark green foliage first changes to purple and then red. The wavy leaves may be 2–5 in (5–12.5 cm) long and oval or elliptical in shape. Fruits hang down from each flower cluster in one to three fleshy drupes, changing from green to dark blue, enclosing a ridged stone, ripening in late fall.

Sweet Crab Apple
Malus coronaria
The dark green leaves are toothed, many with pointed lobes at the base. The fruit is yellow-green and waxy with white flesh surrounding shiny brown seeds, and ripens in October.

Quaking Aspen
Populus tremuloides
The rounded leaves are attached to the branch by a long flattened stem, which leads to the characteristic trembling in the wind. The fruits are 4-inch (10 cm)-long rings of 6 mm-long capsules, each of which has ten tiny seeds that are dispersed by the wind in early summer.

Black Willow
Salix nigra
Long narrow leaves are finely toothed, either dark green on both sides or lighter green on the underside. The fruit is a 6 mm-long capsule that splits open when mature to reveal minute down-covered seeds, which are wind-borne on silky hairs.

American Basswood
Tilia americana
Leaves are heart-shaped, finely toothed, and often lopsided. The larger side of the leaf at the base is palmate but the rest of the leaf is pinnate. A small spherical, downy nutlet develops at the end of every flower, which is perfect, and ripens by late summer.

Sugarberry
Celtis laevigata
The leaves commonly are narrow and smooth with a pointed tip and an uneven, or oblique, base. The small fleshy drupe hangs singly from a slender stem, and is dark purple when it ripens in September and October. It can remain on the branches through winter, but the seeds are dispersed by the birds and rodents that eat and digest it in the tree and on the ground.

American Elm
Ulmus americana
The leaves are oval, double serrated, with an oblique base. The flowers are perfect, with both male and female parts, but they are protogynous: the female parts mature first, which limits self-fertilization. The fruit is a flat elliptical samura with a hairy fringe and a papery wing surrounding the single seed.

Avg height: 50–80 ft (15–24 m)
Avg trunk diameter: 24–36 in (61–91 cm)
Lifespan: 100–250 years

Bark: When young, the bark is smooth, thin, and banded, reminiscent of birch bark. As the tree matures, the bark darkens and becomes rougher to protect the tree from harmful pests and harsh weather. Furrows develop over time, creating cracks in the bark.

Foliage: The ovate-lanceolate leaves are alternately arranged, have finely toothed margins and are 2–5 in (5–13 cm) long. Leaves turn yellow to red in the fall.

Flowers: The flowers bloom from April to May. They are perfect and have five petals that are white and pink-streaked. Drooping racemes reach 4–6 in (10–15 cm) in length each containing several dozen flowers.

Fruit: Abundant drupes—the cherries—are dark reddish to black and 0.25–0.375 in (0.5–1 cm) wide, falling in drooping clusters from the racemes.

BLACK CHERRY
Prunus serotina

Prunus serotina, commonly known as black cherry, rum cherry, black mountain cherry, and wild cherry, is a deciduous tree or shrub. The crown is conical when the tree is young, becoming oval-headed over time with spreading limbs and arching branches. When crowded, the tree will grow tall and slender. The black cherry belongs to the Rosaceae family. *Prunus serotina* is the largest of the native cherry trees. Its epithet comes from the Latin word sero meaning "late," which is in reference to the relatively late flowering and fruiting of this tree compared to other cherries. Wilted leaves are poisonous to livestock, but cherry trees are often abundant on farms, making up entire hedgerows because of the ample light, so it may be necessary to just keep the animals away from the trees.

INTERESTING FACTS

• The Native Americans made a cough syrup that was derived from the bark of the black cherry tree.

• The valuable wood is used to make musical instruments, furniture, children's toys, and paneling.

• The tree is slightly poisonous as it contains traces of cyanide which may cause health issues if ingested. This functions as a defense mechanism against herbivores.

HABITAT AND DISTRIBUTION

Habitat
The black cherry tree grows best in moist, open woods. They are often found along roadsides and open fields where there is sufficient moisture in the soil. They require full sun for best growth. They can be found in upland and lowland woods and along streams.

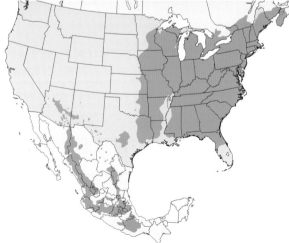

Distribution
The black cherry ranges from southeastern Canada through the eastern U.S. west to eastern Texas. There are disjunct populations in the mountains of the southwestern U.S., central Texas, Mexico, and Guatemala.

Avg height: 60–80 ft (18–24 m)
Avg trunk diameter: 8–10 in (20–25 cm)
Lifespan: 60–100 years

Bark: The bark on younger trees is thin, smooth, and olive-green. As the tree matures, the bark turns gray and thickens, developing deep grooves.

Foliage: The most notable feature of the leaves are the curved teeth on the margins. The leaves are simple and alternate with a flat leaf stalk, which causes them to tremble in the wind. They are oval to broadly egg-shaped with a pointed tip and rounded base, green above and cottony-white below, and 2–4 in (5–10 cm) long and 1.5–3.5 in (3.8–8.8 cm) wide.

Flowers and seeds: Like other aspens, bigtooth aspens are dioecious: male and female flowers are on separate trees. Male catkins are 1–3.5 in (2.5–8.8 cm) long. Female catkins are 1.25–3 in (3.2–7.5 cm) long, but after pollination, lengthen to 4 in (10 cm) and each flower produces light green, curved, slight hairy seed capsules with two chambers, each with 3–9 small seeds .

BIGTOOTH ASPEN
Populus grandidentata

Populus grandidentata, commonly known as bigtooth aspen, large-tooth aspen, white poplar, Canadian poplar, and American aspen, is a straight-trunked deciduous tree with gently ascending branches and a rounded crown. Its name is derived from the Latin words *populus* meaning "poplar," *grandis* meaning "large," and *dentate* meaning "teeth." *Grandidenta* translates to "large teeth," which refers to the distinct ridges on the leaves of this tree, which are commonly called teeth. The bigtooth aspen produces more than a million seeds a year and nearly 80 percent are viable, but very few germinate because they are only viable for two weeks. The bark, foliage, and twig buds are consumed by wildlife, and they are the host species for eastern tiger swallowtail and viceroy larvae.

INTERESTING FACTS

• The light-colored, finely textured wood is used for making structural panels and pulp, as well as ladders, sports equipment, and home construction.

• The bigtooth aspen reproduces rapidly from root suckers and seeds, often invading cleared areas.

• While indifferent to soil conditions, it is plagued by insect problems and disease.

HABITAT AND DISTRIBUTION

Habitat
While the bigtooth aspen is adaptable to a wide range of soils, it grows best on loamy and sandy soils with good drainage. The trees are very shade intolerant and are often pioneer species on disturbed sites.

Distribution
The bigtooth aspen is native to northeastern North America: in the U.S. it is found from Maine south to Virginia and west across the Great Lakes region to Minnesota and Iowa; in Canada, it is native from Nova Scotia west across Quebec and Ontario to southeastern Manitoba. Disjunct populations are found in North and South Carolina, Kentucky, Tennessee, and southern Illinois.

Avg height: 65–80 ft (20–25 m)
Avg trunk diameter: 8–31 in (20–80 cm)
Lifespan: 100–200 years

Bark: The bark of young trees is greenish-white and smooth. As the tree ages, the bark becomes a more chalky white with black patching and furrows that develop at the trunk's base.

Foliage: Leaves are a dark glossy green reaching 3 in (7.6 cm) in length with finely toothed margins. They are ovate-triangular to nearly round and turn a golden yellow in fall.

Flowers and fruit: Quaking aspens are dioecious, with male and female flowers on separate trees, appearing on catkins in spring, gray-green in color. On female trees, the catkins are followed by green conical capsules hanging from the catkins, which split in half when mature, releasing the thousands of tiny cottony seeds.

QUAKING ASPEN
Populus tremuloides

Populus tremuloides, commonly known as trembling aspen, American aspen, popple, white poplar, trembling poplar, golden or mountain aspen, or quaking aspen, gets its name from its leaves, which tremble in even the lightest wind because of their flexible and flattened leaf stalks or petioles. These deciduous trees have tall, straight trunks and a pyramidal crown when young and a rounded, narrow crown once mature. It has the widest geographical distribution of any North American tree. In order to germinate, the seeds must land on a sufficiently moist seedbed within a couple of days of dispersal while they are still viable—which rarely happens; therefore, aspen reproduce far more commonly and successfully by root sprouts.

INTERESTING FACTS

• In wild growing conditions, groups or groves of aspens are often clones of each other, with the trees growing from a single extensive underground root system.

• Aspens are susceptible to a large number of diseases including cankers, powdery mildew, rusts, leaf spots, and dieback, which often causes premature leaf drop.

• Quaking aspen density is greatest in Alaska, Colorado, Michigan, Wisconsin, and Minnesota, with each of these states containing at least 2 million acres (809,371 hectares) of commercial quaking aspen forest

HABITAT AND DISTRIBUTION

Habitat
Populus tremuloides thrive in cool northern climates and struggle in areas with heat and humidity. They grow best in consistently moist, well-drained soils in full sun, although they can tolerate a range of soil types. They are generally intolerant of urban pollutants.

Distribution
The quaking aspen can be found in Alaska and most of Canada, New England, the Pacific Northwest, the Great Lakes, and south in the Rockies to New Mexico and Arizona. Scattered populations occur from Mexico to Guanajuato.

EASTERN COTTONWOOD
Populus deltoides

Avg height: 65–195 ft (20–60 m)
Avg trunk diameter: 10–70 in (27–178 cm)
Lifespan: 70–100 years

Bark: When young, the bark is silvery-white and smooth or lightly fissured. On mature trees, the bark is dark gray and ridged.

Foliage: Leaves are coarsely toothed, acuminate, and triangular. They are glossy and dark green, reaching 1.5–4 in (4–10 cm) in length and 1.5–4.5 in (3–12 cm) in width.

Flowers: Male and female flowers are on separate trees, with tiny flowers that grow in catkins. Male flowers are reddish; female flowers are cream-colored and become seed capsules once they are fertilized.

Seed: The capsules split when ripe, releasing abundant densely tufted seeds with silky white hairs that are distributed by wind.

Populus deltoides has three recognized subspecies: the best known, the eastern cottonwood or necklace poplar, *P. deltoides* subsp. *deltoides*; the Plains cottonwood, *P. deltoides* subsp. *monilifera*; and the Rio Grande cottonwood, *P. deltoides* subsp. *wizlizeni*. Its common name "cottonwood" refers to its abundance of cottony seed pods (samaras), while "necklace poplar" refers to the long, narrow line of seed capsules that resemble a string of beads. However, it is dioecious—the male and female flowers are on different trees—so the seed pods are only produced by the female trees. Its gummy end buds, coarsely toothed leaves, and yellowish twigs distinguish it from other poplars. It is the official state tree of Kansas, Nebraska, and Wyoming.

INTERESTING FACTS

• General Custer fed his horses and mules the bark during the 1868–69 winter campaign against Native American tribes south of Arkansas.

• This tree is susceptible to a wide range of diseases including powdery mildew, rusts, leaf spots, cankers, and dieback.

• The wood is weak and warps easily so it has little commercial value. It is used to make pulp, crates, and plywood.

• It is not suitable for urban areas because the trees are weak-wooded and their roots can damage sewer lines and buckle sidewalks.

HABITAT AND DISTRIBUTION

Habitat
Populus deltoides typically grows along rivers and streams and in swamps and lowland areas. Mud banks left after flooding provide ideal conditions for seedling germination.

Distribution
The eastern cottonwood (Populus deltoides subsp. deltoides) [by the way, subsp. is not italicized] has the broadest range, from southeastern Canada and the eastern U.S., west to North Dakota and south to Texas. The Plains cottonwood (Populus deltoides subsp. monilifera) is native from southcentral Canada, south through the central U.S. to Texas. The Rio Grande cottonwood (Populus deltoides subsp. wislizeni) has the narrowest range: from southern Colorado and Texas, south to northeastern Mexico.

BLACK WILLOW
Salix nigra

Avg height: 30–60 ft (9–18 m)
Avg trunk diameter: 20–30 in (50–80 cm)
Lifespan: 40–100 years

Bark: Young black willow trees have dark brown bark that is smoother than that of mature trees. Once mature, the bark has profoundly furrowed fissures with scaly ridges. These ridges fork near the base of the trunk. Its dark-colored bark gives this tree its name.

Foliage: Leaves are arranged alternately. The leaves are easily detached from the branch and are long and thin, reaching around 5 in (12.7 cm), tapering to a pointed tip. The margins are gently serrated and the leaves are sometimes called a blade due to their long, narrow shape.

Flowers and fruit: Black willows are dioecious—male and female flowers grow on different trees. The yellow, tubular-shaped flowers grow in catkins, They produce small reddish-brown capsules containing tiny, furry seeds. Once mature, the capsules split to release the seeds, which require a wet environment for germination, ideally flooded and waterlogged areas.

The black willow was identified by botanist Humphry Marshal, known as the father of American dendrology (the study of trees). He identified this tree in 1875 and called it the most important tree to the southeastern regions of the United States. Once matured, the black willow is the largest willow in the world. Its name is derived from its dark ebony-colored bark. This tree is part of the willow family *Salicaceae* and is deciduous and fast-growing. The black willow is also known as Goodding's willow, Dudley willow, swamp willow, or southwestern willow; however, these common names may be applied to other species as well. Goodding's willow has been considered either a variety of black willow (*Salix nigra* var. *vallicola*) or a separate species (*Salix gooddingii*).

INTERESTING FACTS

• The wood of the black willow is light and flexible and was at one point used for making artificial limbs.

• Native Americans noted the effectiveness of black willow bark to relieve pain and made good use of it—in fact, it contains salicylic acid, a chemical similar to aspirin (acetylsalicylic acid).

• Because black willows bloom early, they are valuable to wildlife and provide essential nectar for bees emerging from their hives in early spring.

HABITAT AND DISTRIBUTION

Habitat
While the black willow can grow in partial shade, it grows best in full sun. Wet soil is ideal for these trees, which will grow even after severe flooding. They are commonly found near the shores of rivers, floodplains, lakes, or swamps. In cool and moist temperate mixed woods they are one of the dominant species.

Distribution
Black willows extend from southern sections of New Brunswick and Ontario, Canada, to northern Florida. It is native in the deep south, including southern Texas, and north to the Northwoods of Minnesota. It was introduced to western states as a solution to control erosion and now grows in many regions of that area.

AMERICAN BASSWOOD

Tilia americana

Avg height: 60–120 ft (18–37 m)
Avg trunk diameter: 36–60 in (91–152 cm)
Lifespan: 150–200 years

Bark: The bark is light brown to gray with narrow, well-defined fissures. The bark is longitudinally furrowed with narrow ridges, creating a rough texture.

Foliage: Leaves are ovate to cordate, simple, asymmetrical, and alternately arranged. Most are 4–6 in (10–15 cm) long and wide but can grow up to 10 in (25 cm). or even 15 in (38 cm) long and 10 in (25 cm) wide. They are initially pale green and become smooth and dark green when mature. In fall, they are yellow to yellow-green.

Flowers: Flowers grow in drooping, cymose clusters of 6–20. The flowers are fragrant, small, and yellowish-white, up to 0.4–0.5 in (1–1.4 cm) in diameter. The flowers have five sepals and petals and numerous stamens.

Fruit: Flowers are followed by nutlets that are small, hard, cream-colored, and globose, reaching 0.3–0.4 in (0.8–1 cm) in diameter.

Tilia americana, also known as American basswood, American linden, bee tree, or lime tree, or, is a deciduous tree with an ovate-rounded crown. Branches are spreading and often pendulous. The common name of "basswood" is derived from bastwood in reference to the tree's tough inner bark (bast). The common name of "linden" and the name "Linneaus" both derive from the Swedish word lind, which means linden tree. There are some 20 species of *Tilia* across the world, but *Tilia americana* is the only representative of its genus in the Western Hemisphere; some recognize the Carolina linden as one of the many gradations of American basswood with a more southern distribution, while other botanists consider it a separate species, *Tilia carolianiana*.

INTERESTING FACTS

• The bast (inner bark) of the tree has been used to make mats, baskets, fishing nets, and rope.

• A variety of wildlife benefits from this tree. The flowers provide abundant nectar for insects; the seeds are eaten by squirrels, mice, and chipmunks; the bark is eaten by voles and rabbits; and the leaves are eaten by caterpillars.

• The wood, leaves, flowers, and charcoal made from the wood are used for medicinal purposes, including treating headaches, high blood pressure, inflammation, infections, fever, cough, and cold.

HABITAT AND DISTRIBUTION

Habitat
These trees are found in moist, low woods and dry upland areas in acidic soil. They typically occur along streams, on bluff bases and slopes, as well as many other types of woods.

Distribution
The American basswood is native to a variety of habitats from Quebec to the far eastern North Dakota and southeastern corner of Manitoba south to North Carolina, Tennessee, and Oklahoma. There are concentrations along the Ohio River Valley to Missouri and in forested areas of the Appalachian Mountains.

SUGARBERRY
Celtis laevigata

Avg height: 80–100 ft (24–31 m)
Avg trunk diameter: 18–24 in (46–61 cm)
Lifespan: 100–150 years

Bark: The bark is pale and smooth, marked with lighter, corky patches. When the tree is mature, the gray bark develops a warty texture with smooth bark between.

Foliage: Leaves are oblong-lanceolate to ovate with smooth margins and a long, tapering tip. They are glossy to dull and green with mostly uneven leaf bases. The leaves reach 2–4 in (5–10 cm) in length.

Flowers and fruit: In spring, greenish flowers appear with female flowers solitary and male flowers growing in clusters. Female flowers are followed by fleshy, round, berrylike drupes that mature from light green to a deep purple and reach 0.25 in (0.6 cm) in diameter. Each drupe contains one seed.

Sugarberry is a deciduous tree with upright-arching branches and a spreading rounded crown. It is commonly used as a shade tree due to its tolerance of urban stresses and handsome appearance. Its name *Celtis* is a Greek word that means a tree that bears sweet fruits. *Laevigata* means smooth, referring to the tree's smooth leaves. It is commonly known as sugarberry, sugar hackberry, Texas sugarberry, lowland hackberry, palo blanco, or southern hackberry. The common name hackberry refers to the peeling bark of mature trees, as from a distance the peeling bark gives the trees the appearance of being hacked or chopped by an ax. The sugarberry is a member of the elm family and the hackberry genus.

INTERESTING FACTS

• Houma Native Americans used the sugarberry bark to treat sore throats and the Navajo nation used the leaves and branches to make a dark red or brown dye.

• The sugarberry is the host for Hackberry Emperor butterflies.

• The leaves are rich in antioxidant properties.

HABITAT AND DISTRIBUTION

Habitat
Celtis laevigata commonly grows in wet to moist soils in floodplains and along streams. It is commonly found within the floodplains of major southern rivers, in clay soils of shallow sloughs or broad flats.

Distribution
The sugarberry is native to and widely distributed throughout the south-central and southeast U.S.. Its range extends from northeastern Mexico north to Texas and the eastern U.S..

AMERICAN ELM
Ulmus americana

Avg height: 60–100 ft (18–30 m)
Avg trunk diameter: 24–60 in (60–150 cm)
Lifespan: 200–300 years

Bark: The light gray bark and tends to have scaly and deeply furrowed ridges. The fibrous bark has been used as a tying and binding material to make whips or swing ropes.

Foliage: Leaves grow up to 3–6 in (7.5–15 cm) long and 1–3 in (2.5–7.6 cm) wide and are elliptical with toothed edges. The top of the leaf tends to feel rough, like sandpaper.

Flowers: Although the flowers are perfect, they are wind-pollinated because the female parts mature before the male parts, reducing self-fertilization. The tiny flowers completely lack petals, growing in dangling clusters.

Fruit: Elliptical flattened samaras hang from the same stalks as the flowers did, each with a single seed and a papery wing. Brown at maturity, in late spring and early summer, they are are dispersed by the wind.

Ulmus americana, commonly known as American elm, is a species native to eastern North America. This hardy tree can withstand extreme winter temperatures and, when healthy, can live for several hundred years. Beloved for its graceful shape and leaves that turn golden in the fall, the American elm is unfortunately very vulnerable to the Dutch elm disease, which has killed many centuries-old specimens and decimated its population. However, the work of tree geneticists has made disease-resistant trees a reality, improving its once dire prognosis. It is a deciduous hermaphroditic tree that can grow to more than 100 ft (30.5 m) tall and has small, purple-brown apetalous flowers. *Ulmus americana* is not affected by changes in daylight hours so it grows well into the fall.

INTERESTING FACTS

• For almost a century, the American elm had been identified as a tetraploid, which made it unique within the genus. In recent years, however, about 20% of wild American elms have been identified as diploid, with some scientists arguing they may even constitute another species.

• In the 19th and early 20th centuries, *Ulmus americana* was a popular tree for cities, where it was used to line main avenues. Its graceful shape, high tolerance of urban conditions, and rapid growth pattern made it extremely popular across the country, which led to an unhealthy monoculture of elms

HABITAT AND DISTRIBUTION

Habitat The species grows in a wide variety of habitats, particularly rich bottomlands, stream banks, and flood plains. While common on wet flats, it is not restricted to this type of habitat and can also thrive in hillsides and other well-drained soils. In the Appalachian Mountains, it grows along rivers and is limited to the vicinity of large streams. It can grow at an elevation of up to 2,000 ft (610 m) but is difficult to find at higher altitudes.

Distribution
The American elm is native throughout eastern North America, covering a range that extends from Nova Scotia, west through southern Quebec, central Ontario, southern Manitoba, and southeastern Saskatchewan, south from the Dakotas to eastern Texas, along the Gulf Coast east to central Florida, and north along the East Coast to Maine..

INDEX

INDEX

INDEX

Credits

1 ForestSeasons.Shutterstock.com, 2 Joe Sohm | Dreamstime.com, 3 L-R: Saengdao Srisupha | Dreamstime.com, Runa0410/Shutterstock.com, Suzi44/Shutterstock.com, Ufuk ZIVANA. Shutterstock.com, 4 Gary C. Tognoni/Shutterstock.com, 5tr mario95/Shutterstock.com, 5br Scisetti Alfio/Shutterstock.com, 6br1 Waldemarus/Shutterstock.com, 6br2 simona pavan/Shutterstock.com, br3 Catmando Shutterstock.com, 7 Makoto Honda | Dreamstime.com, 8-9tl Andrii Tolstopiatykh | Dreamstime.com, 9tr Joan Carles Juarez/Shutterstock.com, 8-9bl Ezume Images/Shutterstock.com, 9br M. Schuppich/Shuttesrtock.com, 10-11 Sundry Photography/Shutterstock.com, 12-13 Nagel Photography/Shutterstock.com, 14-15 ANGHI/Shutterstock.com, 16-17 Sky Cinema/Shutterstock.com, 18l Iwona Erskine-Kellie/Wikimedia Commons, 18cl Lara Red/Shutterstock.com, 18cr Peter Turner Photography/Shutterstock.com, 18r Nick Pecker/Shutterstock.com, 19l Jack N. Mohr/Shutterstock.com, 19cl Dave Nelson | Dreamstime.com, 19cr Famartin/Wikimedia Commons, 19r SusquehannaMan/Wikimedia Commons, 19t InfoFlowersPlants/Shutterstock.com, 19t Avictorero | Dreamstime.com, 19tl Lukas Gojda/Shutterstock.com, 19t Lukas Gojda/Shutterstock.com, 20cla Deb Merchant/Shutterstock.com, 20clb Walter Siegmund/Wikimedia Commons, 20bl Walter Siegmund/Wikimedia Commons, 20c brewbooks/Wikimedia Commons, 21 Riekefoto | Dreamstime.com, 22tl Bejlui/Shutterstock.com, 22cla Keith Kanoti/Wikimedia Commons, 22bl world of inspiration/Shutterstock.com, 22c Keith A. Spangler | Dreamstime.com, 23 Meunierd | Dreamstime.com, 24lt PHOTCHARA SANGDAO/Shutterstock.com, 24cla sunnychicka/Shutterstock.com, 24cb Walter Siegmund/Wikimedia Commons, 24bl Dave Powell, USDA Forest Service/Wikimedia Commons, 24c Sky Cinema/Shutterstock.com, 25 Alexander Denisenko/Shutterstock.com, 26tl gallofoto/Shutterstock.com, 26cla Steve Baskauf/Wikimedia Commons, 26clb ANGHI/Shutterstock.com, 26bl ChWeiss/Shutterstock.com, 26c Gerry Bishop/Shutterstock.com, 27 SariMe/Shutterstock.com, 28tl mmstudiomk/Shutterstock.com, 28cl Edita Medeina/Shutterstock.com, 28bl Walter Siegmund/Wikimedia Commons, 28c Andy Nowack | Dreamstime.com. 29 Peter Turner Photography/Shutterstock.com, 30tl Catmando/Shutterstock.com, 30cla Orjen.Wikimedia Commons, 30clb Walter Siegmund/Wikimedia Commons, 30bl Lara Red/Shutterstock.com, 30c EWY Media/Shutterstock.com, 31 Iwona Erskine-Kellie/Wikimedia Commons, 32cla S Buwert/Shutterstock.com, 32clb Edita Medeina/Shutterstock.com, 32bl Richard P Long/Shutterstock.com, 32c Walter Siegmund/Wikimedia Commons, 33 Peter Turner Photography/Shutterstock.com, Walter Siegmund/Wikimedia Commons, 34tl Jamy/Shutterstock.com, 34-35 L-R 1st row: Walter Siegmund/Wikimedia Commons, Lukas Gojda/Shutterstock.com, InfoFlowersPlants/Shutterstock.com, Famartin/Wikimedia Commons, Menno van der Haven/Shutterstock.com, 2nd row: Walter Siegmund/Wikimedia Commons, Gedeminas777/Shutterstock.com, S. Rae/Wikimedia Commons, USDA-NRCS PLANTS Database/Herman, D.E. et al., Richard P Long/Shutterstock.com, 3rd row: Walter Siegmund/Wikimedia Commons, Walter Siegmund/Wikimedia Commons, David J. Stang/Wikimedia Commons, 4th row: Nikki Yancey/Shutterstock.com, Lara Red/Shutterstock.com, Thayne Tuason/Wikimedia Commons, Edita Medeina/Shutterstock.com, 36tl Bejlui/Shutterstock.com, 36cla karamysh/Shutterstock.com, 36clb prot3006/Shutterstock.com, 36bl Randy Bjorklund/Shutterstock.com, 36c IrinaK/Shutterstock.com, 37Jessica Ward | Dreamstime.com, 38tl ajdebre/Shutterstock.com, 38cla Walter Siegmund/wikimedia commons, 38clb Steve Estvanik | Dreamstime.com, 38bl Ed Ogle/wikimedia commons, 38c Famartin/wikimedia commons, 39 Mario Krpan | Dreamstime.com, 40tl ajdebre/Shutterstock.com, 40cla Rob Duval/wikimedia commons, 40clb Lukas Gojda/Shutterstock.com, 40bl Jojoo64/Shutterstock.com, 41 ClubhouseArts/Shutterstock.com, 42tl Digital Storm/Shutterstock.com, 42cla MaXX12/Shutterstock.com, 42clb OtiKo/Shutterstock.com, 42bl kosaku1999/Shutterstock.com, 43 Treetime.ca/wikimedia commons, 44tl ajdebre/Shutterstock.com, 44cla Stefan_Sutka/Shutterstock.com, 44clb Nadya So/Shutterstock.com, 44bl1 Kuvatoive/Shutterstock.com, 44bl2 Nadya So/Shutterstock.com, 44c ForestSeasons/Shutterstock.com, 45 AlessandroZocc/Shutterstock.com, 46cla Dana Kenneth Johnson | Dreamstime.com, 46clb blueeyes/Shutterstock.com, 46bl1 Nick Pecker/Shutterstock.com, 46bl2 Nick Pecker/Shutterstock.com, 46c TFoxFoto/Shutterstock.com, 47 Peter Turner Photography/Shutterstock.com, 48tl Maksym Bondarchuk/Shutterstock.com, 48cla Dave Nelson | Dreamstime.com, 48clb Tara Schmidt/Shutterstock.com, 48bl Amelia Martin/Shutterstock.com, 48c Kaye Oberstar | Dreamstime.com, 49 Michael Tatman/Shutterstock.com, 50cla Dave Nelson | Dreamstime.com, 50clb Dave Nelson | Dreamstime.com, 50bl1 Jesse Taylor/Wikimedia Commons, 50bl2 Hellmann1 | Dreamstime.com, 50c Gary Gilardi/Shutterstock.com, 51 Jack N. Mohr/Shutterstock.com, 52tl Kazakovmaksim | Dreamstime.com, 52-53 L-R 1st row: ChWeiss/SShutterstock.com, Walter Siegmund/Wikimedia Commons, Fredlyfish4/Shutterstock.com, Re Metau/Shutterstock,com, torreya_trekker/Wikimedia Commons, Peter Turner Photography/Shutterstock.com, Crusier/Wikimedia Commons, 2nd row: Mav/Wikimedia Commons, Tim Menzies/Wikimedia Commons, ZayacSK/Shutterstock.com, David J. Stang/Wikimedia Commons, David J. Stang/Wikimedia Commons, Peter Leitheiser/Wikimedia Commons, 3rd row: guruXOX/Shutterstock.com, USDA-NRCS PLANTS Database/Herman, D.E./Wikimedia Commons, S. Rae/Wikimedia Commons, Danita Delimont/Shutterstock.com, Marinodenisenko/Shutterstock.com, Tara Schmidt/Shutterstock.com, Hellmann1 | Dreamstime.com, 54tl Flash Vector/Shutterstock.com, 54cla Keith Kanoti/Wikimedia Commons, 54clb Riekefoto | Dreamstime.com, 54bl Nikki Yancey/Shutterstock.com, 54r Rachel Portwood/Shutterstock.com, 55 Gerald D. Tang | Dreamstime.com, 56tl Nadezhda79/Shutterstock.com, 56cla Tracy Immordino/Shutterstock.com, 56clb Fredlyfish4/Shutterstock.com, 56bl Mario Krpan | Dreamstime.com, 56c SA 3.0/Wikimedia.com, 57 Robert L. Anderson/Wikimedia Commons, 58cla BZ Photos/Shutterstock.com, 58clb Nikki Yancey/Shutterstock.com, 58bl Nikki Yancey/Shutterstock.com, 58c Kenraiz/Wikimedia Commons, 59 Nikki Yancey/Shutterstock.com, 60cla Skyprayer2005/Shutterstock.com, 60clb Re Metau/Shutterstock.com, 60bl Re Metau/Shutterstock.com, 60c Kenraiz/Wikimedia Commons, 61 Holly Guerrio/Shutterstock.com, 62cla Zayacskz | Dreamstime.com, 62cla Nikki Yancey/Shutterstock.com, 62bl Nikki Yancey/Shutterstock.com, 62c Robert Waltman | Dreamstime.com, 63 fujifujisakisaki/Shutterstock.com, 64cla Woodlotat/Wikimedia Commons, 64clb torreya_trekker/Wikimedia Commons, 64bl David Edelman | Dreamstime.com, 64c Kseniia Rudova | Dreamstime.com, 65 Andrii Volgin/Shutterstock.com, 66cla Gerald D. Tang | Dreamstime.com, 66clb Peter Turner Photography/Shutterstock.com, 66c COULANGES/Shutterstock.com, 67 Gerald D. Tang | Dreamstime.com, 68cla OSU Special collections/Wikimedia Commons, 68clb Richard Sniezko/Wikimedia Commons, 68c Mitch from Costa Mesa/Wikimedia Commons, 69 Silversyrpher/Wikimedia Commons, 70 clb Danita Delimont/Shutterstock.com, 70bl Richard Sniezko/Wikimedia Commons, 70c brewbooks/Wikimedia Commons, 71 brewbooks Wikimedia Commons, 72cla billysfam/Shutterstock.com, 72clb Structured Vision/Shutterstock.com, 72bl Nikolai Kurzenko | Dreamstime.com, 72c Erich G. Vallery/Wikimedia Commons, 73 billysfam/Shutterstock.com, 74cla Nikki Yancey/Shutterstock.com, 74clb Mav/Wikimedia Commons, 74bl Hellmann1 Dreamstime.com, 74c Mary Key/Shutterstock.com, 75 Steve Heap/Shutterstock.com, 76cla Wilhelm Zimmerling PAR/Wikimedia Commons, 76clb Tim Menzies/Wikimedia Commons, 76bl Elektryczne jabtko/Wikimedia Commons, 76c Mary Key/Shutterstock.com, 77 Mikhail Gnatkovskiy | Dreamstime.com, 78tl Kate Cuzko/Shutterstock.com. 78-79 L-R 1st row: Rhododendrites/Wikimedia Commons, Nikki Yancey/Shutterstock.com, Mario Krpan | Dreamstime.com, Re Metau/Shutterstock.com, David Edelman | Dreamstime.com, Jason Hollinger/Wikimedia Commons, homeredwardprice/Wikimedia Commons.com, 2nd row: Wirestock | Dreamstime.com, M Huston/Shutterstock,com, Breck P. Kent/shutterstock.com, MARINA LOVER/shutterstock.com, Lostafichuk | Dreamstime.com, SusquehannaMan/Wikimedia.com, 3rd row: Nikki Yancey/Shutterstock.com, Nikki Yancey/Shutterstock.com, Richard Sniezko/Wikimedia Commons, Richard Sniezko/Wikimedia Commons, Boyd J English/Shutterstock.com, Amelia Martin/Shutterstock.com, Hellmann1 | Dreamstime.com, 80 cla Gerald D. Tang | Dreamstime.com. 80clb ChWeiss/Shutterstock.com, 80bl Rhododendrites/Wikimedia Commons, 80c Gerald D. Tang | Dreamstime.com, 81 Gerald D. Tang | Dreamstime.com, 82cla twinlynx/shutterstock.com, 82clm Peter Turner Photography/Shutterstock.com, 82clb Korean Botanist/Shutterstock.com, 82c Putneypics on Flickr/Wikimedia Commons, 83 Famartin/Wkimedia Commons, 84cla Dmitrij Opanovich/Shutterstock.com, 84clb Wyatt Greene/Wikimedia Commons, 84bl Mkopka | Dreamstime.com, 84c autrpy-https://www.inaturalist.org/Wikimedia Commons, 85 torreya_trekker/Wikimedia Commomns, 86cla Stephen Puliafico/Shutterstock.com, 86clb Marinodenisenko/Shutterstock.com, 86bl Boyd J English/Shutterstock.com, 86c Boyd J English/Shutterstock.com, 87 meunierd/Shutterstock.com, 88tl Govinda Valbuena/Shutterstock.com, 88cla ForestSeasons/Shutterstock.com, 88clb Michael G McKinnel/Shutterstock.com, 88bl Alicia Pimental/Wikimedia Commons, 88c Famartin/Wikimedia Commons, 89 Woodlot/Wkimedia Commons, 90cla David J. Stang/Wikimedia Commons, 90clb Peter Leitheiser/Wikimedia Commons, 89bl SusquehannaMan/Wikimedia Commons, 89c bobistraveling/Wikimedia Commons, 91 Famartin/Wikimedia Commons, 92l Mario Krpan | Dreamstime.com, 92cl Rosser1954/Wikimedia Commons, 92cr Dcrjsr/Wikimedia Commons, 92r Nina B/Shutterstock.com, 93l Brynn/Wikimedia Commons, 93cl M. Schuppich/Shutterstock.com, 93cr Dietmar Rabich/Wikimedia Commons, 93r/Wikimedia Commons, 93tr Ihor Hvozdetskyi/Shutterstock.com, spline_x/Shutterstock.com, osoznanie.jizni/Shutterstock.com, 94cla Peter Turner Photography/Shutterstock.com, 94clb Ingrid Curry/Shutterstock.com, 94bl Ole Schoener/Shutterstock.com, 94c Zack Frankr/Shutterstock.com, 95 Peter Turner Photography/Shutterstock.com, 96cla Anna Nelidova/Shutterstock.com, 96clb spline_x/Shutterstock.com, 96bl HHelene/Shutterstock.com, 97 Mario Krpan | Dreamstime.com, 98cla AnnaNel/Shutterstock.com, 98clb Famartin/Wikimedia Commons, 98bl Dendro100/Shutterstock.com, 98c John B./

Credits